The Sun of Wisdom

The Sun of Wisdom

Teachings on the
Noble Nagarjuna's
Fundamental Wisdom
of the Middle Way

❖ ❖ ❖ ❖ ❖

KHENPO TSÜLTRIM GYAMTSO

Translated and edited by Ari Goldfield

SHAMBHALA *Boston & London* 2003

Shambhala Publications. Inc.
Horticultural Hall
300 Massachusetts Avenue
Boston, Massachusetts 02115
www.shambhala.com

9   8   7   6   5   4   3   2

Printed in the United States of America

⊗ This edition is printed on acid-free paper that meets the
American National Standards Institute z39.48 Standard.
Distributed in the United States by Random House, Inc.,
and in Canada by Random House of Canada Ltd

Library of Congress Cataloging-in-Publication Data
Khenpo Tsultrim Gyamtso, Rinpoche, 1934–
The Sun of Wisdom: teachings on the noble Nagarjuna's
fundamental wisdom of the middle way/Khenpo Tsultrim
Gyamtso. — 1st ed.
p. cm.
Includes index.
ISBN 1-57062-999-4 (pbk.)
1. Nagārjuna, 2nd cent. Madhyamakakārikā—Commentaries.
2. Mādhyamika (Buddhism) I. Nagārjuna, 2nd cent.
Madhyamakakārikā.
BQ2797 .K54 2002
294.3'85—dc21
2002152104

Contents

Translator's Preface

ON HIS TEACHING TOUR of Europe and the United States in 2000, Khenpo Tsültrim Gyamtso Rinpoche chose to explain the noble protector Nagarjuna's great treatise *The Fundamental Wisdom of the Middle Way*[1] on several occasions. Rinpoche's style was to select important verses from each chapter as the basis for what in Tibetan is called a *chi don*, an overview explanation of the entire text. Rinpoche based his teachings on the commentary to the text by Ju Mipham Rinpoche[2] entitled *A Jewel of the Powerful Nagarjuna's Intention That Perfectly Illuminates the True Nature*.[3] I had the great fortune to serve as Rinpoche's translator when he gave these teachings.

In response to the many requests from students that Rinpoche's explanations of *The Fundamental Wisdom of the Middle Way* be published in written form, Rinpoche directed that this book be compiled from the teachings he gave on the text at three different Dharma centers: Tekchen Kyetsal in Spain, Karma Ling in France, and Karmê Chöling in the United States.

In the publication of this book, thanks are due first and foremost

---

1. Tib. *dbu ma rtsa ba shes rab*; Skt. *Mula-madhyamaka-karika*.
2. Ju Mipham Rinpoche (1846–1912) was a great master of the Nyingma lineage of Tibetan Buddhism and one of the leading figures in the *Ri-me* (nonsectarian) movement that began in Tibet in the middle of the nineteenth century.
3. Tib. *dbu ma rtsa ba'i mchan 'grel gnas lugs rab gsal klu dbang dgongs rgyan*.

to Khenpo Rinpoche for giving these impeccable teachings in his inimitably masterful, lucid, warm, and humorous style, which students all over the world have come to appreciate so much. His kindness is immeasurable.

Many thanks also to Drupon Khenpo Lodrö Namgyal and Acharya Sherab Gyaltsen Negi for their brilliant and patient word-by-word explanations in 1998 of Mipham Rinpoche's commentary; to Elizabeth Callahan, Claudine Mona, Tingdzin Ötro, and the transcription staff at Karmê Chöling for graciously providing the tapes and transcripts of Rinpoche's teachings, which served as the basis for this book's contents; to Jim Scott for so expertly translating and arranging Jetsün Milarepa's song of realization, *An Authentic Portrait of the Middle Way*, as well as most of the songs of realization that Khenpo Rinpoche quoted from during the teachings, which are reprinted in this book with only a few minor revisions that attempt to reflect the particular explanations Rinpoche gave of the songs at the time; and to Emily Bower, Joanne Burgess, Tracy Davis, Larry Mermelstein, and Claudine Mona for their most helpful editorial advice.

May all who read this book find it of some benefit to their understanding of the profound nature of genuine reality, and may the merit of that be a cause for all sentient beings to awaken into complete and perfect enlightenment. Until that happens, may everything be auspicious, and may the teachings of the genuine Dharma flourish in a world filled with happiness, harmony, and peace.

Ari Goldfield
Dharamsala, India
November 2001

Introduction

WHATEVER ACTIVITY WE ENGAGE IN, our motivation is very important. According to the tradition of Mahayana (Great Vehicle) Buddhism, the motivation we should cultivate is *bodhichitta*—the mind turned toward supreme enlightenment. One way to do so is to think first of our father and mother in this lifetime, and then extend the love and compassion we feel for them to all sentient beings, including even our enemies. It is the case that all sentient beings, including our enemies, have been our own father and mother countless times, and therefore they have been indescribably kind to us countless times. The greatest thing we can do to repay sentient beings' kindness is to lead them all to the state of complete and perfect enlightenment, the state of buddhahood, and in order to do this, we must listen to, reflect upon, and meditate on the teachings of the genuine Dharma with all the enthusiasm we can muster. This is the supreme motivation of bodhichitta—please give rise to it as a first step whenever you read, reflect on, or meditate upon the teachings in this book.

The topic of this book is the text known as *The Fundamental Wisdom of the Middle Way*, composed by the noble protector Nagarjuna. Nagarjuna is a special teacher in the history of Buddhism. The Buddha himself prophesied that Nagarjuna would be born four hundred years after the Buddha's own passing and that he would give vast and perfect explanations of the Buddha's teachings. Nagar-

juna fulfilled this prophecy both as a teacher of many students who
went on to become great masters themselves and as an author of
texts that expound and clarify the meaning of the Buddha's words.
Buddhists and non-Buddhists alike have studied these texts from
Nagarjuna's time to the present.

Nagarjuna's commentaries form three main collections of texts
that explain, respectively, the Buddha's own three series of teachings
known as the three turnings of the wheel of Dharma. Thus, in the
set of compositions known as *The Collections of Advice,* Nagarjuna's
focus is the first turning of the wheel. He describes how a human
life gives one the invaluable opportunity to practice the Dharma;
how this life and everything one knows of and experiences within it
are impermanent; how samsara—the cycle of existence in which
confused sentient beings endlessly wander from one lifetime to the
next—is characterized by constant suffering, in both gross and
subtle forms; and how practicing the Dharma leads to the attainment of nirvana, the state of liberation that transcends samsara's
suffering once and for all. This is a brief summary of the teachings
the Buddha gave in his first turning of the wheel of Dharma. These
are teachings from the perspective that appearances truly exist in
just the way they seem to—that the individual, the individual's past
and future lives, the suffering the individual experiences in samsara,
and the liberation the individual can attain in nirvana all exist in
precisely the way they appear.

In the middle and final turnings of the wheel, the Buddha described the true nature of reality, explaining that the way things
appear to be is different from the way they actually are. The Buddha
taught that of all the progressively subtle ways of explaining the true
nature of reality, the ultimate description one can make is that the
true nature of reality is the true nature of mind, the union of luminous clarity and emptiness. It is difficult, however, to understand
what "the union of luminous clarity and emptiness" means as an
initial statement, and therefore the Buddha taught about the two
aspects of emptiness and luminous clarity separately and in great

detail in the sutras of the middle and final turnings, respectively. Once students understand what emptiness is, and then what luminous clarity is, they can then much more easily understand how it is that genuine reality is in fact the union of the two.

Nevertheless, the profundity and vastness of the Buddha's teachings in the sutras make them difficult for ordinary individuals to understand. For this reason, Nagarjuna composed *The Six Collections of Reasonings* to explain the middle turning's *Sutras of Transcendent Wisdom* (the *Prajñāpāramitā Sutras*), and *The Collection of Seventeen Praises* to explain the final turning's *Sutras on the Buddha Nature*. From among *The Six Collections of Reasonings*, the major text is *The Fundamental Wisdom of the Middle Way*.

WHAT IS THE MIDDLE WAY?
Since it is a commentary on the middle turning of the wheel of Dharma, the main topic of *The Fundamental Wisdom of the Middle Way* is emptiness. In fact, the terms *Middle Way* and *emptiness* are synonyms. *Middle Way* means that the true nature of the phenomena we experience lies in the middle, between all possible extremes that can be conceived of by the intellect. The true nature of reality cannot be described by any conceptual fabrication, by any conventional term or expression. Thus, it is not existent, not nonexistent, not something, not nothing, not permanent, not extinct; it is not the lack of these things, and it is not even the middle in between them, for that is a conceptually fabricated extreme as well. The true nature of reality transcends all the notions we could ever have of what it might be. This is also the ultimate understanding of the second turning's description of emptiness. Emptiness ultimately means that genuine reality is empty of any conceptual fabrication that could attempt to describe what it is.

The path leading to the direct realization of this inconceivable, genuine nature of reality begins with gaining certainty in this profound view of emptiness. This is an essential first step because it is not enough just to read the teachings that say, "All phenomena are emptiness; the nature of reality is beyond concept," and, without knowing the reasons these teachings are accurate, to accept them on blind faith alone. If we do, we will not remove our doubts, and our mere opinion that the teachings are valid will not do us any good when these doubts come to the surface. When we gain certainty in the teachings on emptiness, however, then it will be impossible for doubts to arise.

The way that Nagarjuna helps us to gain such certainty is through the use of logical reasoning. This is particularly important for us in this day and age, when academic inquiry, science, and technology are at the forefront. At the dawn of the twenty-first century, people are very well educated and are used to using their intelligence to examine and understand things. Nagarjuna's method is perfectly in harmony with this—he teaches us how to determine the true nature of reality for ourselves by logically analyzing the things that appear to us. By analyzing in this way we can gain stable certainty in the profound view. Many of Nagarjuna's logical reasonings negate the true existence of things and conclude that things do not truly exist, that they are empty of inherent nature. This leads some people to think that Nagarjuna's view is nihilistic—he negates actors, actions, causes and results, the Buddha, and everything else in samsara and nirvana. What then is left of our experience? What is the use or meaning of life if everything is empty in this way?

THE THREE STAGES OF ANALYSIS

It is therefore very important to know that the Buddha taught about the nature of reality in three stages. First, in order to teach his disciples that positive actions lead to happiness and negative actions lead to suffering, the Buddha taught about these things as if they were real. In order to help disciples give rise to renunciation of samsara and longing for nirvana, he taught about samsara's suffering and nirvana's liberation from that suffering as if they were real. Furthermore, since all of these teachings depend upon the existence of a self, the Buddha taught about the self, who performs positive and negative actions and experiences their results, who wanders from lifetime to lifetime in samsara, and who can gain the liberation of nirvana, as if it were real. This was the first stage of the teachings, the teachings of the first turning of the wheel, called the stage of no analysis—no analysis of the true nature of the phenomena about which the Buddha taught.

The second stage reflects the fact that once students gain confidence in the law of cause and result and develop renunciation of samsara and longing for nirvana, it is then important that they reverse their clinging to themselves and these phenomena as being truly existent, because this clinging actually prevents them from gaining the liberation for which they strive. In the second stage, therefore, the Buddha taught that phenomena do not truly exist. For example, in the *Heart of Wisdom Sutra*, the Buddha taught, "There is no eye, no ear, no nose, no tongue, no body, no mind," and so forth. This second stage is called the stage of slight analysis— the point at which phenomena are analyzed and found to be lacking in inherent nature, to be empty of any truly existent essence.

In this way, we can see that we need the teachings on nonexistence to help us reverse our clinging to things as being existent. The true nature of reality, however, transcends both the notion of existence *and* that of nonexistence. Therefore, in the third stage, the stage of thorough analysis, the Buddha taught that we must also give up our clinging to nonexistence if we are to realize the simplicity, the freedom from all conceptual fabrications, that is reality's ultimate essence.

The Buddha taught these latter two stages in the middle turning of the wheel of Dharma. Of the two philosophical schools whose explanations are based on this middle turning, the Middle Way Autonomy school (Svatantrika Madhyamaka) emphasizes the second stage, that of slight analysis, whereas the Middle Way Consequence school (Prasangika Madhyamaka) emphasizes the third stage, that of thorough analysis. The Autonomy school refutes true existence and asserts emptiness to be the true nature of reality; the Consequence school refutes true existence but does not assert anything in its place, because its proponents recognize that to do so would obscure realization of the freedom from all conceptual fabrications that is the true nature of reality itself.

The Fundamental Wisdom of the Middle Way teaches from the perspectives of both the second and third stages, and therefore both the Autonomy and Consequence schools find their roots in this text. It is important for us to identify what stage a particular teaching in the text is coming from so that we can link it with the explanations of one of these two schools and also understand its intended purpose. If it is a refutation of existence, its purpose is to help us overcome our clinging to things as being real; if it teaches the freedom from all conceptual fabrications, it is intended to help us understand how reality is actually beyond all our concepts of what it might be.

DEPENDENTLY ARISEN MERE APPEARANCES

Understanding these three stages of the Buddha's teachings highlights one of the main differences between the Middle Way view that Nagarjuna teaches and the view of nihilism. A nihilistic view would have a strong clinging to the notion of nonexistence, whereas in the third stage, the Middle Way explains that the nature of reality transcends both existence *and* nonexistence.

A nihilistic view would also completely deny the existence of past and future lives, the law of cause and result, the rare and supreme Buddha, Dharma, and Sangha, and so forth. The Middle Way does not fall into that extreme, however, because it does not deny that all these things—in fact all the outer and inner phenomena that compose samsara and nirvana—exist as dependently arisen mere appearances. The best example to help us understand what this means is the moon that appears on the surface of a pool of water. When all the conditions of a full moon, a cloud-free sky, a clear lake, and a perceiver come together, a moon will vividly appear on the water's surface, but if just one condition is absent, it will not. Thus, the moon has no independent power to decide to appear—it appears in the water only in dependence upon the coming together of these causes and conditions. At the same time, it appears, however, it is just a mere appearance, because it is empty of true existence—not the slightest atom of a moon can be found anywhere in the water. Thus, the water-moon is a mere appearance of something that is not really there. In the same way, all the phenomena of samsara and nirvana appear due to the coming together of causes and conditions, and at the same time as they appear, precise knowledge (*prajñā*) that analyzes their true nature cannot find the slightest trace of their actual existence. They are appearances that are empty of any substantial essence, just like water-moons, but just like water-moons, their emptiness of essence does not prevent them from appearing vividly when the proper causes and conditions come together. This is the truth of dependent arising, the union of appearance and emptiness that is the essence of the Middle Way view. It frees the Middle Way from the extreme of realism, because it does not superimpose true existence onto the nature of genuine reality where there is none, and from the extreme of nihilism, because it does not deny that things appear due to the coming together of causes and conditions.

Gaining certainty in this view is incredibly beneficial, because such certainty helps us to begin to eradicate the root cause of our suffering—our confused tendency to cling to things as being truly existent. As a result of thinking that things truly exist, we become attached to things we like, averse to things we do not like, and stupidly indifferent to everything else. Such experiences of attachment, aversion, and stupidity are called the mental afflictions (*kleshas*), and when we come under their influence, our minds become agitated and we accumulate karma, meaning that we think confused thoughts and perform confused actions in a constant attempt to get the things we like and avoid the things we dislike. The only result, however, of all our confused struggles to gain happiness and avoid suffering is to become further enmeshed in the mental afflictions, in hope and fear, and in the suffering of losing or not getting what we like and of meeting up with what we do not wish for.

If, however, we can see that things are not truly real—that they are mere appearances whose true nature is beyond all concepts of what it might be—then our experience of both good and bad events in life will be open, spacious, and relaxed. When something good happens, we will be able to enjoy it in a relaxed way, free of clinging to it and free of the fear of it departing. When something bad happens, if we recognize its true nature, we will be relaxed within it and our minds will be undisturbed. In short, realizing the true nature of reality brings inner peace—genuine happiness and ease that outer conditions cannot disturb. As the lord of yogis Milarepa describes it in a vajra song of realization called *An Authentic Portrait of the Middle Way*, also included in this book, appearance-emptiness is "a union vast and spacious," and realizing that this is the true nature of reality brings the experience of genuine reality's natural openness and spaciousness. The enlightened masters of the past have all described this experience of realization in precisely this way, and some of their songs appear in this book to give you an idea of what this direct experience of reality is like. By gaining certainty in emptiness, instead of accumulating the causes of suffering, you will accumulate the causes of gaining this very realization that Milarepa and all other enlightened masters have achieved.

Our current confusion and the prospects of liberation from it are illustrated well by the example of dreams. When we dream and do not know that we are dreaming, all the forms, sounds, smells, tastes, and tactile sensations we seem to perceive on the outside, and all the thoughts we seem to have on the inside, appear to be real; we believe they are real, and we have further experiences that seem to confirm to us that they are real. As a result, we experience the turmoil of attachment to things in the dream that we find pleasing and of suffering when we think something or someone is harming us, even though all the while there is nothing really there at all. If we can simply recognize that we are dreaming, however, then all that trouble just vanishes. We see that all the images that appear in the dream—appearances of clean and dirty, good and bad, friend and enemy, happiness and suffering, and everything else—are all mere appearances that are not real. They are actually of the nature of perfect equality—there is really no difference between them at all. We see that the true nature of all of these appearances is beyond all concepts of what it might be. Then, whatever good or bad appears to happen, since we know that it is just a dream, we know that we do not need to fixate on it—we can just experience whatever it is in a way that is untroubled by the mental afflictions, in a way that is open, spacious, and relaxed. We can even do things like fly in the sky.

Like dream appearances, the daytime forms, sounds, smells, tastes, and tactile sensations we perceive on the outside, as well as our thoughts and mental states within, are all mere appearances that are empty of inherent nature, that do not truly exist. Appearing while empty, empty while appearing, all the phenomena we experience are the union of appearance and emptiness, like dreams and illusions. The more you understand this, the less troubled you will be by the mental afflictions—in fact, even when mental afflictions and suffering arise, you will be able to know that they too are illusory, and they will gradually lose their strength and dissolve. You will gain deeper and deeper insight into the genuine nature of reality beyond concept, insight that will become more and more subtle and will eventually transform into the wisdom of direct realization.

WISDOM AND COMPASSION TOGETHER

The Mahayana path that leads to the state of complete and perfect enlightenment, however, is not just the path of wisdom realizing emptiness alone—it is rather the path that combines wisdom and compassion together. In fact, the easiest way to understand what it means to attain "complete and perfect enlightenment," or buddhahood, is to know that it is the state one achieves when one has taken one's wisdom realizing emptiness to its ultimate degree and one's compassion for others to its ultimate degree. Upon achieving that level, one has the greatest motivation and ability to be of benefit to others, and, putting that ability into action in a truly infinite way, one performs limitless benefit for others and naturally benefits one-self at the same time. Therefore, cultivating compassion for others is an essential component of Mahayana practice.

How should we cultivate compassion? From among the many different methods the Buddha taught, all of which are important for us to train in, the one that is particularly connected with the view of the Middle Way is this: Understanding that reality is appearance-emptiness, one cultivates compassion for those sentient beings who suffer because they mistakenly believe that appearances, particularly appearances of suffering, are truly existent. As Milarepa once sang, "I see this life to be like an illusion and a dream, and I cultivate compassion for sentient beings who do not realize this."

This is the answer to the question raised above: From the per-spective of the Middle Way's teachings on emptiness, what is the meaning or purpose of life? The purpose is to follow Milarepa's example by, first, continually training in the view that sees that all our experiences in this life are dependently arisen mere appearances whose true nature is beyond conceptual fabrications, is open, spa-cious, and relaxed; and second, cultivating compassion for all sen-tient beings who suffer as a result of not realizing that this is the genuine nature of reality. We should do whatever we can to help others on a conventional level, for example, by practicing generosity toward those in need and taking care of those who are sick; and at the same time we should continually make aspiration prayers that in the future we will be able to help all sentient beings realize the true nature of reality, because when they do so it will most definitely liberate them from samsara's ocean of suffering once and for all. In order to help them gain this realization that is the one certain anti-dote for suffering and the one certain bestower of happiness, we need to gain it ourselves, which we do by studying, reflecting, and meditating upon the teachings on the true nature of reality contained in such extraordinary texts as *The Fundamental Wisdom of the Middle Way*. Dedicating ourselves in this way to training on the Mahayana path of wisdom and compassion together, whose fruition is the attainment of buddhahood, and which is of infinite benefit to limitless sentient beings, is the greatest purpose we could ever have.

ABOUT THIS BOOK

The Fundamental Wisdom of the Middle Way is composed of twenty-seven chapters. Each is itself a commentary on a different statement made by the Buddha in the sutras comprising the second turning of the wheel of Dharma. Nagarjuna proves the validity of the Buddha's teachings with logical reasoning. The chapters also answer the successive arguments put to Nagarjuna by those who believed that things truly exist. In each chapter, Nagarjuna would successfully refute one such argument; his opponents would then come up with another argument that they thought proved that things were real, and Nagarjuna would refute that, and so on—that is why there are twenty-seven chapters! They are all very beneficial to us because they help us to overcome our own doubts, the same doubts that Nagarjuna's opponents had.

Some of the chapters are long and the logical reasonings they present are quite detailed. This book examines the most important verses from each chapter. It is necessary to proceed in this way because very few people today have the time to study the entire text. People in modern times need concise Dharma teachings that are profound, easily understandable, and readily applicable to daily life. By reading, contemplating, and meditating on the teachings in this book, you will get to the heart of Nagarjuna's text in a direct way that will greatly enhance your precise knowledge of the genuine nature of reality.

There are similarities from one chapter to the next in the methods of logical inference and reasoning used to help you gain certainty in emptiness. This similarity of method makes it easier for you to gain facility with these logical reasonings, and will also help you to see how wonderfully applicable they are to such a great variety of subjects. By reviewing these same basic reasonings as they apply to different subjects, your familiarity with them will grow and you will gain more and more certainty in their conclusions. Emptiness is the deepest and most subtle topic one could ever attempt to understand, so it is never enough to hear or read teachings on emptiness just once. Rather, we must analyze them again and again, apply them again and again, and continually cultivate familiarity with their profound meaning.

Along these lines, this book also includes other selections of texts that will help to deepen your understanding of emptiness and strengthen your certainty. The first is the *Heart of Wisdom Sutra,* one of the Buddha's most concise teachings on emptiness, yet incredibly powerful and profound. This sutra was actually spoken by the great bodhisattva Avalokiteshvara, but since he did so through the power of the Buddha's blessing, it is considered to be the very speech of the Transcendent Conqueror himself. By analyzing the nature of reality with your intelligence in the way that Nagarjuna describes, you will gain stable certainty in the teachings of this sutra. Furthermore, seeing the similarity between the teachings of the Buddha and those of Nagarjuna will increase your confidence in Nagarjuna's words.

Also included here are the verses that describe the twenty emptinesses from the text by the glorious Chandrakirti[4] called *Entering the Middle Way,* itself a commentary on the meaning of Nagarjuna's *Fundamental Wisdom of the Middle Way.* Actually, within emptiness itself there are no distinctions between different types of emptiness because emptiness' true nature transcends all concepts that differentiate between one thing and another. Therefore, from the perspective of genuine reality, emptiness cannot actually be divided into twenty different categories or classifications. When the Buddha taught the twenty emptinesses, however, he did so from the perspec-

---

4. A great Indian master of the Middle Way Consequence school.

tive of the twenty different types of phenomena whose various appearances we cling to as being truly existent. Going through the twenty emptinesses helps us to free ourselves from this clinging step by step. The first sixteen emptinesses are the extensive presentation, and these are then summarized into four. Studying Nagarjuna's reasonings makes the twenty emptinesses easy to understand, and at that point Chandrakirti's verses will be a great help to your meditation practice. You can use these verses to practice analytical meditation by reciting the verses describing a particular emptiness and using the logical reasonings Nagarjuna presents to help you come to certainty in the verses' meaning, and then practice resting meditation by simply resting in that certainty that your analysis has produced. You can repeat this process as many times as you like. Machig Labdrön, the greatest woman practitioner in the history of Tibet, taught her students to meditate on the twenty emptinesses in this way as a method to help them realize *prajñāpāramitā*, the transcendent wisdom that realizes emptiness, that is called the Great Mother of all enlightened beings.

Finally, as mentioned earlier, this book includes the vajra song of the lord of yogis Milarepa called *An Authentic Portrait of the Middle Way*. This is one of Milarepa's most important songs because it teaches from the common perspective of the Autonomy and Consequence schools' views. If studying this great text by Nagarjuna, the basis of the Middle Way, leads you to wonder about the Kagyü tradition's particular perspective on these matters, you will find the answer by referring to this song of Milarepa, one of the founders of the Kagyü lineage. *An Authentic Portrait of the Middle Way* is a short song, but it contains a meaning that is profound and vast. It teaches that all of the phenomena of samsara and nirvana do not truly exist and yet they still appear—there is a mere appearance of things, and that appearance is the union of appearance and emptiness. Therefore, it is very helpful to read or sing this song, to memorize it, and to meditate on its meaning. That will be a very good connection for you to make with the profound view of the lineage and the one who realized it perfectly, Milarepa.

Milarepa was the one yogi in the history of Tibet who was universally acknowledged to have attained buddhahood in a single life. If you have faith in him, then singing or reciting his *Authentic Portrait* as you study Nagarjuna's teachings will be of great benefit, because it will help you to overcome your fear of emptiness. If you already have certainty in emptiness, then singing the songs about emptiness that were sung by the realized masters will cause your certainty to grow greater and greater.

In general, all the verses in this book are excellent supports for developing your precise knowledge of genuine reality through study, reflection, and meditation. You should recite them as much as possible, memorize them, and reflect on them until doubt-free certainty in their meaning arises within. Then you should recall their meaning again and again, to keep your understanding fresh and stable. Whenever you have time, use them as the support for the practices of analytical and resting meditation. If you do all of this, it is certain that the sun of wisdom will dawn within you, to the immeasurable benefit of yourselves and others.

Opening Homage

I prostrate to the one
Who teaches that whatever is dependently
    arisen
Does not arise, does not cease,
Is not permanent, is not extinct,
Does not come, does not go,
And is neither one thing nor different things.
I prostrate to the perfect Buddha, the supreme
    of all who speak,
Who completely dissolves all fabrications
    and teaches peace.

❊ ❊ ❊ ❊ ❊

THIS VERSE OF HOMAGE with which Nagarjuna begins the text
explains why it is that we should have such great respect for the
Buddha. Why is the Buddha worthy of our prostration? It is because
the Buddha teaches that all of the phenomena of samsara and nirvana are dependently arisen mere appearances, and that therefore
their true nature transcends the concepts of arising and ceasing, of

permanence and extinction, of coming and going, and of being one thing or different things.

In fact, essential reality (*dharmata*) transcends all conceptual fabrications, and the Buddha taught this to his disciples very clearly. In this way the Buddha taught the path that dissolves all conceptual fabrications and thereby leads to the peace that is free from samsara's suffering. Suffering comes from taking things to be real—from taking friends and enemies to be real, from taking birth and death to be real, from taking clean and dirty to be real, and from taking happiness and pain in general to be real. The Buddha taught that the true nature of reality actually transcends all these concepts—it is the equality of all these seeming opposites—and he also taught us how to realize this. Since putting the Buddha's teachings into practice leads to the complete transcendence of suffering and the perfect awakening of the omniscient enlightened mind, then these teachings are the greatest words ever spoken, and the Buddha himself is the supreme of all who speak. For these reasons, the Buddha is worthy of our respect and our prostration.

1

An Examination of Causal Conditions

In the *Sutra Requested by Madröpa*, the Buddha said:
Whatever arises from conditions does not arise.
It does not have the nature of arising.
Whatever depends on conditions is explained to be empty,
And to know emptiness is the way to be conscientious.

❋ ❋ ❋ ❋ ❋

IN THIS CHAPTER, Nagarjuna explains the meaning of this passage and proves its validity with logical reasoning. The reason Nagarjuna composed this chapter was that people believe that causal conditions are real. As a result of that, they believe that things really happen. They believe that arising is real. When they believe that, it is difficult for them to believe in emptiness and to gain confidence that all phenomena are empty of inherent existence. However, in order to understand the true nature of reality, we must realize that nothing ever really happens. We must realize that arising and birth are not real. Therefore, Nagarjuna analyzes causes, conditions, and arising, and he proves that they are in fact empty of any inherent nature.

Let us begin by looking at this verse spoken by the Buddha. Whatever thing it might be in samsara or nirvana, it can come into existence only in dependence upon its specific causes and conditions. There is nothing that can arise; there is no event of arising at all that can occur without the presence of these causes and conditions to make it happen. This holds for the arising of all the impure phenomena of samsara and all the pure phenomena of nirvana. Whatever arising it is, it can occur only in dependence upon a specific gathering of causes and conditions. Otherwise it will not take place.

Furthermore, whatever arises in dependence upon causes and conditions does not truly arise. One way to understand this is to see that it is not the case that just one single cause or one single condition can bring something into existence, but rather, that many causes and conditions must come together for any one particular result to arise.

Thus, if we look at any particular result and first see that it requires a number of causes and conditions to come together to produce it, we can then look at those causes and conditions and see that each one of them as well requires an incredible number of causes and conditions to cause it to arise. We can go back and back and get to even the most subtle causes and conditions, and we find that these too do not exist independently, but rather can only exist in dependence upon a multitude of their own causes and conditions. Then we realize that nothing exists independently with a nature of its own, that there is nothing truly there. Everything is like a dream and an illusion.

The same can be said for all of the thoughts that arise in our minds, whether they are good thoughts, bad thoughts, or neutral ones. There is not a single thought that can arise on its own, that can decide to come to existence and then be born. Thoughts can arise only when many causes and conditions come together to produce them. Since these causes and conditions also exist only in dependence upon their own causes and conditions, and those causes and conditions themselves need their own causes and conditions in order to arise, and on and on, all of them are empty of inherent existence. The arising of thoughts is therefore empty of any inherent nature.

In this way, we can see that whatever arises in dependence upon causes and conditions is empty of true existence because it does not really arise at all. To know this emptiness is the best way to be conscientious. The reason for this is that everything we experience in this life is appearance-emptiness; however, if we think it is real, we can try very hard to be conscientious, but in fact our confusion about the basic nature of our experiences will make us careless. On the other hand, those who gain stable certainty that their experiences are appearance-emptiness, and are therefore no more real than illusions, correctly understand the true nature of things, and even if they appear to us to be careless, they are in fact more conscientious than anyone!

The first verse of this chapter reads:

Not from self, not from other,
Not from both, nor without cause:
Things do not arise
At any place, at any time.

This verse proves that things do not arise because they do not arise from any of the four extremes: They do not arise from themselves, from something other than themselves, from both themselves and something other than themselves, and they do not arise without any cause at all. These are the only four possible ways in which things could arise, and since none of them are valid, things do not truly arise. Therefore, things do not truly exist.

Why do things not arise from themselves? If they did, the term *arising* would be meaningless. When something is said to arise, this means that it comes into existence anew. However, if things arose from themselves, they would have to first exist in order to then arise from themselves! What would be the point of saying that something "arose" after it was already existent? Why would it have to arise at that point? That is one flaw in this argument.

Another flaw in this position is that if things did indeed arise from themselves, their arising would never end. This is the case because if things arose after they already existed, what would stop their arising? What we observe in the world is that the process of arising stops when the thing that has arisen fully exists. As described above, however, if things arose from themselves, they would have to exist first in order to be there to produce themselves. They would have to arise again even after they existed. They would exist, then arise, then exist, then arise, and what would ever stop them from needing to arise again and yet again? Arising would thus go on forever.

Things do not arise from something different from themselves, either, because if they did, they would arise from things that were not their causes as well as from things that were their causes. Here, when we say that two things are different from each other, it means that they have no connection between them—they are separate and completely independent entities. They are like a horse and a cow.

Therefore, if things arose from other things that were completely separate and independent from themselves, they would be able to arise from anything at all. No connection or relationship would be necessary for one thing to be able to produce another. Darkness would arise from fire, barley would grow from wheat seeds, and so forth. There would be no reason this could not happen, because different things would be arising from different things.

Another reason things do not arise from something different from themselves is that if they did, cause and result would have to exist at the same time. For two things to be different from each other, there have to be two things to begin with. If there is only one thing, what is it different from? Take the example of a seed and a sprout. If the sprout truly arises from the seed that is different from itself, then the sprout and seed would have to exist simultaneously in order to be different from each other. If only one existed at any one time, it would not have the other one there to be different from itself.

However, cause and result do not coexist—they are sequential. When the seed exists, the sprout does not, and when the sprout exists, the seed does not. Therefore, the seed and the sprout cannot be said to be different from each other because only one exists at a time. They never exist simultaneously, so no comparison between them can ever be made. We cannot say that they are two different things because there are never "two" there together—there is only one of them present at any one time. The sprout therefore cannot be said to arise from a seed that is different from itself, and in this way, arising from other is refuted.

The third possibility is that things arise from both themselves and something other than themselves. The problem with this is that all the faults inherent in the first two positions accrue to this third one. Combining wrong view number one and wrong view number two does not erase the faults of the first two views—it just combines them together into doubly wrong view number three.

The fourth possibility is that things arise without any cause at all. If they did, however, then they would either always arise or never arise. This would be the case because the arising of things would not be related to causes and conditions. Thus, a result would always arise because, since its arising would not depend on causes and conditions, it would arise whether its causes and conditions came together or not; or it would never arise because, since it would not have any relation to its causes and conditions, even if they came together they could not produce it.

Furthermore, if things arose without cause, then all the effort people in the world put into bringing things into being would be in vain. Why would farmers plant seeds if harvests would arise without any cause? We can thus see that this fourth possibility is refuted by our own direct experience of the world.

Arising, therefore, does not occur in any one of these four possible ways, and therefore it is not real. What then is the nature of the arising that we see happening in the world all the time? It is mere appearance, just like the arising that appears to happen in dreams. As long as we dream and do not know that we are dreaming, we believe that the arising we see happening in the dream is real. As soon as we recognize that we are dreaming, however, we know that the arising is just a mere appearance that has no reality to it at all. In terms of the ultimate nature of the dream, it transcends both notions of "real" and "false"—it is the equality of real and false that transcends conceptual fabrication.

The same is true for daytime appearances of arising. When we do not analyze them, they appear to be real and we think they are real. At the level of slight analysis, we can apply the reasonings described above and find that the arising is not real after all—it is just mere appearance. Finally, at the level of thorough analysis, we discover that the true nature of arising transcends existence and nonexistence—it is the equality of both. This is how the three stages of no analysis, slight analysis, and thorough analysis apply to the arising that appears in daytime and in dreams.

In the tradition of Mahamudra, the profound set of instructions that describe the true nature of mind and how to meditate upon it, it is explained that mind does not arise, abide, or cease. It is from analyzing in the way that is described in this chapter that you can come to understand that. The same is true for suffering—suffering does not arise from any one of the four extremes, and therefore it does not really happen. It does not truly arise, remain, or cease. However, because of our confused belief that suffering does truly occur, we think that we suffer, while in fact we really do not.

Along these lines, in his song *No Birth, No Base, and Union,* the lord of yogis Milarepa sang:

The true nature of appearances is that
    they've never been born.
If birth seems to happen, it's just clinging,
    nothing more.
The spinning wheel of existence has neither
    a base nor a root.
If there is a base or root, that's only a
    thought.

It is important to know what Milarepa taught about these things. The very identity of what things are is that they never happen; they never come into existence. Then what is happening when we seem to perceive things arising? It is just our clinging, our mistaken perception of something that is not really there. Similarly, the nature of samsara's cycle of existence is that it has no ground, no identifiable basis, support, or origin. When we believe there is some basis or root of our existence, it is only our own confused thoughts that believe it, and nothing more than that.

It is very important to separate the way things appear from the way they truly are. As long as we do not do that, we will continue to think that our confused mode of perception is valid, and we will never gain liberation from the suffering that this confusion causes us. We have to begin to see that the true nature of reality is not as it superficially appears to us to be.

2

An Examination of Coming and Going

In the *Sutra Requested by the Bodhisattva "Shining Intelligence,"* the Buddha taught:

Form does not come and it does not go.

❄ ❄ ❄ ❄ ❄

IN THIS CHAPTER, Nagarjuna proves the validity of this statement with logical reasoning.

Nagarjuna composed this chapter in answer to those who claimed, "Things are not of the nature of emptiness because they come and go—we see them coming and going all the time, so how could they not exist?" This is how it is for confused sentient beings: We see things coming and going, we think this coming and going is real, and we have experiences that seem to confirm to us that coming and going are real. As a result of these three occurrences, we conclude that phenomena are not empty of true existence. Thus, it was necessary for Nagarjuna to demonstrate that coming and going are not truly existent in order to help his opponents, and us as well, to understand that things are actually of the nature of emptiness.

These three occurrences—that coming and going appear to be real, that we then think they are real, and that we have further experiences with regard to them that seem to confirm our belief that they are real—are not enough to prove that coming and going truly exist. All of these things happen in dreams, for example, and yet the coming and going that appear in dreams are not real at all. Similarly, they happen in illusions, in movies, with e-mail, and with watermoons. All of these examples of empty forms demonstrate that just because something appears to be real, that does not prove that it is.

Think of all the shapes and colors, all the different forms that appear to us in dreams. Whatever it might be that appears in the dream, it did not come from anywhere, and it does not go anywhere. Similarly, all of the sentient beings in all of the six realms of samsara do not come from anywhere, and they do not go anywhere. If the beings in samsara came from somewhere else, then they would have to come from somewhere that is not samsara, meaning that they would have had to come from nirvana to samsara, and then they would go back to nirvana. That is not how it is, however—the beings in samsara did not come from nirvana to samsara, so they did not come from anywhere, and therefore they are not going anywhere either. The true nature of sentient beings is empty of coming and going.

Since sentient beings themselves neither come nor go, then this must also be the case for sentient beings' ignorance and their mistaken belief in the true existence of the self, which are the roots of cyclic existence, as well as for the mental afflictions arising from these and the suffering that comes from the mental afflictions. These are all things that really do not come from anywhere and do not go anywhere. Their nature transcends coming and going.

In the *Prajñāpāramitā Sutras*, the *Sutras of Transcendent Wisdom*, the Buddha taught that all phenomena are of the nature of emptiness because they are empty of coming and going. For example, in the *Heart of Wisdom Sutra* the Buddha stated:

> There is no ignorance nor any ending of ignorance.

Ignorance does not truly exist because it does not come from anywhere and it does not go anywhere, and since it actually does not exist in the first place, there can be no real ending of it either.

The first verse from this chapter reads:

> On the path that has been traveled, there is
>   no moving,
> On the path that has not been traveled,
>   there is no moving either,
> And in some other place besides the path
>   that has been traveled and the path that
>   has not,
> Motions are not perceptible in any way
>   at all.

When we ask the question "Does movement really happen?" then we have to look for movement on the path where it would happen if it did actually exist. When we do, we can say that in fact there is no movement along this path, because there is no movement on the part of the path that one has already traveled; there is no movement on the part of the path that one has yet to travel; and in between those two, there is no place where you can see any movement happening at all. For these three reasons, therefore, there is no such thing as motion.

The first reason, that there is no motion on the path that one has already traveled, is valid because we have already crossed that part of the path. There is nothing happening there by definition because one has already moved along that part of the path. There is no longer any movement possible there.

The second reason is also valid. There is no motion on the path one has yet to traverse because movement there has not arisen yet. No motion has happened there yet because one has not yet been there. So there is no motion there either.

The third reason is also valid—that is that no motion is observable on some part of the path that one has neither traversed nor not traversed. The reason for this is that no such part of the path exists—there is no such place that one either has not already been or has yet to go. Besides the part of the path that one has already been on and the part that one has not been on yet, there is nothing in between. If we divide the path into these two parts, we cannot find any third part. Therefore, there is no motion there either.

Similarly, besides the motion that has happened in the past and the motion that has not happened in the future, there is no present motion; there is no action of moving. Someone may say, "There is motion after all, because there is the present movement of the legs walking." Actually, though, that motion is just mere appearance, because in between the motion that has already happened and the motion that has yet to happen, there is no present moment of motion—you just cannot find it. For example, think of your finger moving back and forth. At any one point in time, in between the movement that has already happened and the movement that has yet to happen, you cannot find even the tiniest instant in which motion could occur. Thus, whatever point in time you are looking at you cannot find any present motion, if you think about it in this subtle way. There is no moving of the finger because in between the motion that has already happened and the motion that has yet to happen there is no present movement.

Snap your fingers and see if you can find the finger snap as it is happening. Is it happening in the present? When you snap your fingers, is that the present or the past? The first finger snap that has happened is the past—it is already over. The second snap has not happened yet, so that is the future. And in between these two, there is no present moment of the finger snap.

This is not an examination dealing with things on a coarse level; it is an examination that is looking at things from the perspective of the most subtle moments of time. For example, when we look at a finger snap, that moment can be divided into sixty-four individual units or instants, and those are said to be the most subtle moments of time in terms of what can actually be measured. But we can even go further than that. We can examine even these most subtle moments and see that they too are composed of millions of billions of tinier instants, and each of those instants is composed of an infinite number of subinstants, until finally we realize that there is no truly existent moment of time at all—there simply is no such thing as a "present moment." Thus, since there is no time in which motion could occur, in genuine reality it does not occur. There is no coming, no going.

Since it is the case that in genuine reality phenomena neither come nor go, that their true nature is beyond coming and going, it is also the case that our suffering neither comes from anywhere nor goes anywhere. The same is true of our mental afflictions—our attachment, aversion, pride, jealousy, and stupidity—they neither come from anywhere nor go anywhere. Finally, all of our thoughts— no matter how profound or noble, no matter how vile or base—do not come from anywhere or go anywhere.

It is important for us to apply our understanding that things neither come nor go to these three things: our suffering, our mental afflictions, and our thoughts. Just as appearances in dreams, experiences in dreams, and thoughts in dreams neither come from anywhere nor go anywhere, so it is with all phenomena, and it is in this way that we have to analyze. For example, if it were the case with our suffering and our mental afflictions that some evil spirits were sending them into us, then they would in fact come from to us somewhere else. If there were some creator who was sending all of these bad experiences into us, then again they would come from somewhere else to where we are. Neither of these is the case, however, and therefore suffering, mental afflictions, and thoughts do

not come to us from somewhere else, and they do not go anywhere
when they are finished with us. Nevertheless, it is still the case that
there are superficial appearances, mere appearances of these things,
which arise due to the coming together of causes and conditions.
This is why in his *Song of the Profound Definitive Meaning Sung on
the Snowy Range*, the lord of yogis Milarepa sang:

> When you're sure that conduct's work is
>   luminous light,
> And you're sure that interdependence is
>   emptiness,
> A doer and deed refined until they are
>   gone—
> This way of working with conduct, it works
>   quite well!

In this verse, Milarepa sang of his certainty that appearances arise
in dependence upon the coming together of causes and conditions,
and at the same time they appear, they have no inherent nature—
their nature is emptiness. We have to apply ourselves to gaining the
same certainty that Milarepa did.

Therefore, we have to take this analysis of things that shows they
neither come nor go and apply it to our suffering, our mental afflictions, and our thoughts and see that these three things do not come
or go. To put this into verse:

> While we look with our eyes and it seems
>   that things come and go,
> When we analyze with intelligence, we
>   cannot find any coming or going at all.
> Therefore, know that coming and going are
>   like dreams and water-moons.

A water-moon is a very good example to refer to in this analysis of
coming and going. If a water-moon is shining on a lake and you

walk around the lake to the right, due to the coming together of certain causes and conditions, the moon appears to follow you to the right. For your friends who are walking around the lake to the left, however, due to other causes and conditions, the moon appears to be following them to the left! And for your friends who are just standing still, the moon appears to be motionless. All the while, though, there is no moon that is moving at all. In this way, at the same time that things appear to come and go due to the coming together of causes and conditions, in reality there is no coming or going at all. To put this into verse:

> When we analyze with intelligence, we
>   cannot find any suffering;
> Nevertheless, suffering is something we
>   directly experience.
> Therefore, know that suffering is
>   appearance-emptiness, just like suffering
>   in a dream.

When you gain certainty that the suffering that appears is empty of coming and going, the suffering will dissolve all by itself, and you will experience its true nature, which is open, spacious, and relaxed.

3

An Examination of the Sources of Consciousness

In the *Sutra of the Great Mother Prajñāpāramitā*, the Buddha taught:
The eye is empty of the eye.

❋ ❋ ❋ ❋ ❋

THERE ARE THREE VERSIONS of the *Great Mother Prajñāpāramitā Sutras*: the extensive, middle, and concise editions. The extensive, or great, sutra has one hundred thousand verses and encompasses twelve volumes. The meaning of the passage quoted here from the longest version is that the eye with which we see is empty of inherent nature. It is empty of its own essence.

Just as the eye is empty of its own essence, so the ear is empty of its own essence, and the nose, tongue, body, and mind are all the same—all six inner sources of consciousness (*ayatanas*) are empty of their own essence; they are all empty of what they appear to be.

In Karmapa Rangjung Dorje's *Mahamudra Aspiration Prayer*, the
second line of the ninth verse reads:

As for mind, there is no mind! Mind is empty of essence.

This expresses a very similar meaning: Mind has no inherent nature;
it is empty of true existence.

It is the same with the six outer sources of consciousness: Form
is empty of form, sound is empty of sound, smell is empty of smell,
taste is empty of taste, tactile sensation is empty of tactile sensation,
and phenomena that appear to the mental consciousness are empty
of themselves as well. The example that helps us to understand this
more clearly is when these twelve sources of consciousness appear
in a dream. When the twelve sources of consciousness appear in
dreams, they are dependently arisen mere appearances that are
empty of themselves, empty of being anything, empty of any inherent nature. This is what we have to think about.

The *Heart of Wisdom Sutra* teaches that there is "no eye, no
ear, no nose, no tongue, no body, no mind; no form, no sound,
no smell, no taste, no tactile sensation, no phenomenon"—going
through all of the twelve sources of consciousness. It does not use
the exact same language as the passage from the *Sutra of the Great
Mother* quoted here, but its meaning is the same. Therefore, the
meaning of the statement "There is no eye," for example, is not that
there is no appearance of the eye, but rather that the eye that appears is empty of essence.

You may be familiar with the life story of the great Tibetan *siddha*
Machig Labdrön.[5] She was the fastest reader in the history of Tibet.
In Tibet there is a tradition of reading all the volumes of the Buddha's teachings on special occasions in monasteries, nunneries, or
the homes of sponsors. A good reader can read one volume in a

---

5. *Siddha* means "one who has gained accomplishment." It refers to the great Buddhist practitioners who have gained direct realization of the true nature of reality.

day; someone who is exceptionally fast can read three volumes in a day. Well, Machig Labdrön could read all twelve volumes of the extensive *Great Mother Prajñāpāramitā Sutra* in a single day, which she did on one occasion for thirty days in a row. When she did this, she read, for example, that form, the first of the six outer sources of consciousness, is not white, it is not red, it is not rectangular, it is not circular—form is empty of inherent nature. As a result of reading this again and again, she realized emptiness directly and became known as the Prajñāpāramitā siddha, the siddha who realized emptiness by means of the *Prajñāpāramitā Sutras*. After she passed away, her son, Gyalwa Döndrup, sang a song in which he praised her for this incredibly unique feat, because while most other siddhas gain realization through Vajrayana[6] practices, she was able to do so from simply reading the *Prajñāpāramitā Sutras'* descriptions of emptiness. In honor of her accomplishment, Gyalwa Döndrup praised her as "Mother, Prajñāpāramitā siddha-mother." Thus we can see that it is indeed possible to realize the nature of reality by gaining an understanding of emptiness. By meditating on emptiness, if we become skilled at it, we too can become siddhas.

Nagarjuna composed this chapter in answer to those who argued that phenomena are not empty, that they truly exist, because each of the six inner sources of consciousness perceives its respective object among the six outer sources of consciousness. For example, they would say, "This flower exists because my eyes perceive it." Thus, in order to help these people overcome this mistaken belief, Nagarjuna analyzes the sources of consciousness and demonstrates that they do not truly exist after all.

In the course of his analysis, Nagarjuna asks, "If these six inner and six outer sources of consciousness truly exist, then how do they exist in terms of their time sequence?" There are three possibilities: first, that the inner perceiving sources of consciousness exist before the objects they perceive; second, that the perceived objects exist

---

6. Vajrayana, or "adamantine vehicle," is the set of Mahayana practices that is kept secret.

before the subjects that perceive them; and third, that the perceiving subjects and perceived objects come into existence simultaneously.

In fact, all three of these possibilities are logically impossible. The perceiving subject cannot exist before the perceived object, because then there would be a perceiving subject without any object to perceive. Similarly, it cannot be that the perceived object exists before the perceiving subject, because a perceived object cannot exist if there is no subject perceiving it—the term *perceived object* necessarily implies the presence of a perceiver. Thus, the perceiving subject and the perceived object cannot exist sequentially.

They also cannot come into existence simultaneously, because two things that exist simultaneously cannot have any connection or relationship with each other. They cannot have the relationship of being cause and result, for example. This is because something that arises simultaneously with something else has no opportunity to be that second thing's cause. It only arises at precisely the same time as its supposed result, so how could it have produced that result? It would have had no time to do so. It can therefore only be that things that arise simultaneously do so independent of each other.

In this case, it would be impossible for the perceived object and the perceiving subject to be unrelated in the way that two things that come into existence simultaneously are unrelated, because the perceived object and perceiving subject are cause and result—the cause for there being a perceiving consciousness is that there is an object to perceive. If they arose simultaneously, however, they could not have such a relationship, because the perceived object would have no opportunity to cause the perceiving consciousness to arise.

Thus, we see that in fact there is no way that the inner and outer sources of consciousness can truly occur, because they cannot occur sequentially, they cannot occur simultaneously, and there is no other possibility. So then what are they? They are mere appearances, like illusions, like e-mail, and like movies. They have no true existence.

Snap your fingers and then analyze by asking, "What comes first, the finger snap or the ear consciousness perceiving it?" We have to analyze based on our own experience, so how did they happen? Did the finger snap come first? Or did the ear consciousness perceiving the finger snap come first? Or did the finger snap and the ear consciousness perceiving it occur at the same time?

The snap you perceived could not have come before the consciousness that perceived it, or else there would have been a perceived object without any perceiver of that object. Similarly, the consciousness that perceived the finger snap could not have come first because then it would have preceded the finger snap that it perceived. Finally, the consciousness perceiving the finger snap and the finger snap could not have truly occurred simultaneously, because if they did, they would have been unrelated entities—the finger snap would not have been the cause of the arising of the consciousness that perceived it. Thus, they did not exist sequentially, they did not exist simultaneously, and there is no other possibility. Your finger snap and the consciousness that perceived it, therefore, were dependently arisen mere appearances that did not truly exist.

This is an analysis using logical reasoning that Nagarjuna first applies to the eye seeing forms, but, as we have just seen, it is also applicable to the ear hearing sounds and to all the other sense experiences as well. The verse that explains this is the eighth in the chapter:

> Know that these reasonings refuting the
>   faculty that sees
> Refute the faculties that hear, smell, taste,
>   touch, and the mental faculty as well,
> Refute the hearer and the other perceiving
>   consciousnesses,
> Refute sound and the other perceived
>   objects.

Sometimes it might seem as if the object exists before the consciousness that perceives it. For example, when we light a candle in the morning, we might come back a little while later and see the candle again, so it seems that the candle flame existed before our perception of it. That is not really the case, however, because what we are doing in that situation is mixing together all of the moments of the continuum of the candle flame and thinking that they are all the same thing. They are not just one thing, though, because each moment is completely individual, different from every other moment; each individual instant of the candle flame arises only in dependence upon its own independent set of causes and conditions, then ceases, and then is replaced by a completely different candle flame in the next instant. Thus, the individual moments of flame arising and ceasing one after the other in succession are not all the same thing, but rather they are many different things that only look alike, which is why it is so easy to mistake them for being just one thing. So the candle flame we perceive when we walk back into the room did not exist for even the slightest instant before the moment we perceived it to be there. In the same way, whenever we talk about a perceived object, whatever it is, we are talking about something whose existence is only momentary, perceived by an equally momentary consciousness. Analyzing in this subtle way helps us to see why an object that is perceived cannot exist before the consciousness that perceives it.

We can also look at the case of a father and his son and see that the father cannot really exist before the son, the son cannot exist before the father, and they cannot come into existence simultaneously either, so they too cannot be real. If we asked people, "Who comes first, the father or the son?" everyone in the world would answer, "The father comes first." The reason people would say that is that they mistake an entire continuum of separate instants for one thing. If it were really the case that the father existed first, then the man would have been a father *before* the birth of his son, and even when that man was a little boy he would also have had to be a father. That is not the case, though, because every instant in the continuum of his existence is different from all the other instants.

We have to see how it is that we confuse individual entities in a continuum for one thing, how these confused appearances exist in accordance with worldly convention, and then we have to distinguish this confused way things appear from the way things actually are, which we can determine with logical analysis.

Thus, the father cannot exist before the son, because if he did, he would be a childless father. The son cannot exist before the father, because if he did, he would be a fatherless son. They cannot exist simultaneously either, because if they came into existence at the same time, one would have no opportunity to bring the other into existence. Therefore, they do not truly exist. They are not real. Then what are they? They are mere appearances that arise due to the coming together of causes and conditions, like dreams, water-moons, and rainbows. Their true nature transcends conceptual fabrications. It is open, spacious, and relaxed.

4

An Examination of the Aggregates

❊ ❊ ❊ ❊ ❊

THE FIVE AGGREGATES (*skandha*s) are everything included in matter and mind. To describe them briefly, the aggregate of *forms* comprises all material phenomena. In sentient beings, this refers to each individual's body; it also generally includes all matter, all objects of sense perception that exist in the outside environment.

The aggregate of *feelings* is defined as our experiences of sensations that we find pleasant, unpleasant, or neutral.

The aggregate of *discriminations* is defined as "clinging to characteristics" and refers to all of our thoughts that things are either clean or dirty, hot or cold, good or bad, and so forth.

The aggregate of *formations* includes all the other thoughts and emotions that individuals experience. Some of them are positive, like faith, nonviolence, and joyous diligence; some are negative, like anger, jealousy, and arrogance; some could be either positive or negative, like regret or analysis. This aggregate also includes the entities that are the phases of the existence of what is material and mental, like arising, abiding, cessation, and so forth—the stages that matter and mind pass through.

Finally, the aggregate of *consciousnesses* refers to the six primary consciousnesses that perceive the essence of their respective objects: the eye, ear, nose, tongue, and body sense consciousnesses, and the mental consciousness.

In the *Heart of Wisdom Sutra*, Shariputra asked Avalokiteshvara, "How should noble men and women who wish to engage in the profound practice of transcendent wisdom train?" By the power of the Buddha's blessing, Avalokiteshvara was able to respond in the following way:

> Shariputra, noble men and women who wish to engage
> in the profound practice of transcendent wisdom should
> see this clearly: They should see clearly that the five ag-
> gregates are empty by nature.

In another passage in the *Prajñāpāramitā Sutras*, the Buddha taught:

> Form is empty of form.

In this chapter, Nagarjuna proves the validity of these statements with logical reasoning.

Nagarjuna composed this chapter in answer to those who claimed that the aggregates truly exist because the Buddha explained them in his Abhidharma teachings.[7] The Buddha described them

---

7. The Abidharma is a set of the Buddha's teachings from the first turning of the wheel of Dharma in which he described the characteristics of, among other things, the sources of consciousness, aggregates, and elements. In these teachings, the Buddha did not explicitly refute the true existence of the phenomena that he described. He did explicitly refute their true existence, however, in the teachings of the second turning of the wheel.

and therefore they must exist. It then must be the case, they argued, that the twelve sources of consciousness, the subjects of Nagarjuna's refutations in the last chapter, also exist, because the twelve sources of consciousness are included within the five aggregates. Therefore, the five aggregates exist, the twelve sources of consciousness exist, and things are not empty after all—they are real. To help these people understand that this is not the case, that things are actually empty of true existence, Nagarjuna had to demonstrate that the five aggregates do not truly exist. This is his focus in this fourth chapter.

The problem with the way that those who assert that things exist thought about things was that they thought that if you say things exist—if you use the word *existence*—it necessarily implies *true* existence. According to the proponents of the Middle Way, however, things in conventional reality exist as dependently arisen mere appearances. Therefore, to say that conventional appearances exist does not imply that they are real—they are simply mere appearances that occur due to the coming together of causes and conditions, like dreams, illusions, movies, and water-moons.

Out of the five aggregates, Nagarjuna analyzes the aggregate of forms because, since it is the coarsest of the five aggregates, it is the easiest to examine. The way he does so is to break down the aggregate of forms into its causal and resultant constituents. Thus there are causal forms, which consist of the four great elements of earth, water, fire, and wind, and resultant forms, consisting of the five sense faculties and the five objects they perceive—the results that arise from different combinations of the causal forms. Nagarjuna breaks forms down into these two categories and then looks at how these two could possibly exist in relation to each other.

In the preceding chapter Nagarjuna broke down the sources of consciousness into perceived objects and perceiving subjects. Here, he looks at the aggregates in terms of causes and results, and so we can see that there are many different ways one can analyze things.

The root verse that sets out the position of this chapter is the first one:

Except for there being the cause of form,
Form would not be seen.
Except for there being what we call "form,"
The cause of form would not appear either.

If the aggregate of forms truly existed, then the causal forms—the
four great elements, and what results from those four elements—the
five sense faculties and their five objects, would have to exist in
relation to each other in one of the following ways: The cause would
have to exist before the result, the result would have to exist before
the cause, or cause and result would have to exist simultaneously.
We need to examine each of these possibilities to see if any one of
them is viable. If in fact none of them is logically possible, then we
can conclude that forms do not really exist at all.

The first possibility is impossible, because a cause cannot exist
before its result. If it did, why would it be a cause? Something is a
cause only if it produces a result, but if no result exists, then there
is no reason to call anything a cause—nothing has performed the
function of a cause, and therefore no cause exists. Thus, the cause
cannot exist before the result. Nor can the result exist before the
cause, because if it did it would be a result that was not produced
by anything. It would be a result that had no cause. Finally, cause
and result cannot come into existence at the same time, they cannot
exist simultaneously, because two things that come into existence at
the same time do not have a chance to be cause and result—one
does not have the opportunity to produce the other. Things cannot
have a cause-and-result relationship if they occur simultaneously.
Since when we analyze we find that they cannot occur sequentially
and they cannot occur simultaneously, we can definitively conclude
that causal and resultant forms do not truly exist. The appearances
of them are just like the appearances we perceive in our dreams.

Just as we have analyzed forms in this way and have determined
that they do not truly exist, that they are mere appearances of things
that are not really there, like dreams and illusions, so we can analyze

everything else that is included in the four remaining aggregates, as
Nagarjuna explains in verse seven:

> Feelings, discriminations, formations,
> Minds, and all the things there are
> Are susceptible to the same stages of
>   analysis
> That forms have been put through here.

What this verse tells us to do is to analyze feelings, discriminations, formations, and consciousnesses in the same way that we analyzed forms. In the same way as we showed that causal and resultant
forms cannot truly exist, because it is logically impossible for them
to exist either sequentially or simultaneously and there is no third
alternative, so we should examine everything else and see that whatever causes there are, whatever results there are, they cannot truly
exist either.

We can analyze all different kinds of opposites in this way as well.
For example, what comes first, darkness or light? Clean or dirty?
Happiness or suffering? Which one of these really comes first?

Based on this analysis, we can gain certainty that dependently
existent phenomena do not truly exist because they cannot exist one
before the other, they cannot exist simultaneously, and there is no
other possibility. Nevertheless, there are still appearances of them,
mere dependently arisen appearances, like appearances in dreams.
Since there certainly are these appearances, we have no reason to
think that reality is complete nothingness. We have no reason to be
afraid. We should not be afraid of emptiness, because emptiness
does not mean complete nothingness. The true nature of reality is
appearance-emptiness inseparable.

In this same chapter, Nagarjuna also describes the experience of
debating the teachings on emptiness. What is it like when someone
tries to challenge the Middle Way explanations of emptiness in a
debate? The eighth verse reads:

> When emptiness comes up for debate,
> Whatever answers try to prove true
>   existence,
> Those answers are unsound
> Because they are equivalent to the very
>   thesis to be proved.

What happens first is that the ones who follow the Middle Way, who have understood the true nature of reality, encounter people who believe that things truly exist. When this happens, it is necessary for the followers of the Middle Way to explain emptiness to these people who think that things are real. It is also necessary to debate with them. Debate is a good way to bring out the doubts and wrong views held by people who think that things are real.

In the debate, first the people who believe that things really exist try to prove that their position is accurate, and then the proponents of the Middle Way demonstrate that the reasons these people think things really exist are not valid after all. Then the people who believe that things are real come back with answers for why they still believe that. Whatever example they try to give for things being real, however, it is not an example of things being real at all—it is in fact an example of emptiness. Whatever answer they try to give, it is not a valid answer because it is just as empty as what they are trying to prove. Whatever they say, therefore, actually does not prove their point; it proves the Middle Way's point. The reason for this is that they cannot find an example of anything that truly exists. That is the problem they have.

For example, the people who want to say that things truly exist will point to lots of things that seem real, like rocks, diamonds, and mountains. For the proponents of the Middle Way, however, rocks, diamonds, and mountains just prove their own point because they are just as empty as everything else. They can be analyzed with the same reasonings we have used in this chapter that examines forms, and in this way they can be demonstrated to be as empty as anything else.

The people who want to prove that things truly exist have the problem that all phenomena are equally in need of proof of their existence. So whatever these people use as their proof of existence, it is just as in need of proof as the object whose existence they are using it to establish! For example, if someone says, "This table exists because I see it with my eyes," then what proves the existence of the eyes? They cannot say, "My eyes exist because they see the table," because the table's existence is what they were trying to prove in the first place. So they just end up in a circular loop. Furthermore, the experience of seeing a table occurs in a dream, too, and just as the appearance of it in the dream does not prove that it is real, so the appearance of it during the daytime cannot establish its true existence.

In the ninth verse, Nagarjuna shows how it is that those who say that things truly exist cannot find any flaws in the explanations of emptiness:

> When explanations are given about
>   emptiness,
> Whoever would try to find faults in them
> Will not be able to find any faults at all,
> Because the faults are equivalent to the very
>   thesis to be proved.

Here, we are looking at the time when emptiness is being taught. After the teaching is given, someone might criticize the view of emptiness, saying, "If things are empty, then that means that there are no past and future lives. There is no such thing as cause and result. There are no mental afflictions or enemies, and there is no suffering in samsara or liberation in nirvana. Even the three rare and supreme ones, the three precious jewels, do not exist."[8]

8. The *three rare and supreme ones* or the *three precious jewels* refer to the Buddha, Dharma, and Sangha—the three objects of refuge in the Buddhist tradition. One goes for refuge from the suffering of samsara to the Buddha, the teacher; the Dharma, the teachings to be put into

The proponents of the Middle Way would respond to each of these criticisms by saying, "You are right! All the things you name—past and future lives, cause and result, mental afflictions, enemies, suffering, samsara, nirvana, and the three rare and supreme ones—do not truly exist because they are empty of their own essence." Thus, whatever someone claims is a fault in the Middle Way view is in fact empty of its own essence, and so it is precisely equivalent to the thesis that the Middle Way teachings have been proving all along. Since all faults are themselves of the nature of emptiness, it is impossible to find any valid criticisms of the Middle Way teachings on emptiness.

It is important to note here that while all things are empty of true existence, they do still appear, and no one would deny this. Therefore, appearances are described as being mere appearances: While empty they appear, and while appearing they are empty, like dreams, illusions, and water-moons.

This has been a brief explanation of the essential meaning of the fourth chapter of this text. When you read and reflect upon these explanations of the chapters of *The Fundamental Wisdom of the Middle Way*, you will know whether you are gaining certainty in emptiness or becoming more afraid of emptiness. It will be clear to you. Fearlessness of emptiness is a quality that one gains on the third of the four levels of the path of junction, the level of patience.[9] When one gets to that point, one becomes truly unafraid of empti-

practice; and the Sangha, the community of noble practitioners who have directly realized the true nature of reality and who serve as one's guides along the path.

9. According to the Mahayana, there are five paths that constitute the journey to and attainment of enlightenment: the paths of accumulation, junction, seeing, meditation, and no-more-learning. The first two are the paths of ordinary individuals, the next two are traversed by noble bodhisattvas who have directly realized the true nature of reality, and the fifth is the path of the buddhas themselves.

The path of accumulation has three stages and the path of junction four, and although they are both the paths of ordinary individuals, the difference between practitioners at the different stages of these paths is great. For example, achieving only the second level of the path of accumulation brings one certain types of clairvoyance and miraculous powers. The point here is that the attainment of the level of patience on the path of junction is a most wonderful feat indeed.

ness. Before that, however, we still have fear of emptiness, so we need to be on the lookout for that.

The reason that people who believe in the existence of things get frightened of emptiness is that they think the word *emptiness* means that there is absolutely nothing at all, that there is a complete vacuum, and this is frightening. In order to counteract that fear, it is immediately taught that there are the mere appearances of things—that emptiness does not mean a wipeout of everything we perceive and experience. Emptiness refers, rather, to the inexpressible, inconceivable reality that is the essence of all our perceptions and experiences. We can meditate on emptiness and try to cultivate this understanding of it, but if our meditation does not have a lot of power to it, the reason is that we do not have certainty in emptiness yet. And as long as we still have lots of doubts, our meditation on emptiness will not be very helpful.

As Gendun Chöpel[10] explained, we can examine with our intelligence and see that things do not really exist, but then, if we get stuck with a needle, we will have this very vivid experience of existence, and we will think, "Well, maybe there really is something there after all." Thus, when we analyze with logical reasoning, we can gain certainty that things do not truly exist, but we still keep having experiences in which things seem to be so real, contradicting the results of our earlier analysis. This is why it is so difficult to gain certainty in emptiness.

If we did not have all of these experiences that seem so real and if we were not so certain that things exist, then understanding emptiness would be easy. We would not need to study it so much; we would not require so many explanations of it. However, because we believe so strongly in the existence of things and because we keep having all of these experiences that seem to confirm our belief that things are real, it is difficult for us to gain certainty in emptiness. This is why we need to study emptiness so much after all. It is just

10. One of the greatest scholars of modern times, Gendun Chöpel lived from 1902–1951.

as if we had a dream and we did not know that we were dreaming. If someone in the dream came up to us and said, "None of this is real. It does not really exist," we would not easily believe it.

The tradition of Nagarjuna is not the tradition of simply generating a belief or an opinion that things are empty and then proceeding to meditate on the basis of that. It is rather the tradition of cultivating in meditation the certainty that one has achieved through logical analysis. If you study this text in the stages in which it is laid out, its chapters that are the twenty-seven examinations of the emptiness of different subjects, then your certainty in emptiness will definitely grow broader, deeper, and stronger, and your meditation will be much more powerful.

5

An Examination of the Elements

In the *Prajñāpāramitā Sutras*, the Buddha taught:

The element of earth has no nature of its own.

❖ ❖ ❖ ❖ ❖

THIS IS THE ONLY LINE that Mipham Rinpoche quotes in the commentary; in the sutras the Buddha made similar statements about the other elements (*dhatus*)—water, fire, wind, space, and consciousness—and thus he explained the emptiness of the elements in a vast way. In this chapter, Nagarjuna proves the validity of these teachings with logical reasoning.

Those who believed that things actually exist claimed that since the Buddha taught about the elements and their characteristics, they must in fact exist. Furthermore, since the sources of consciousness and the aggregates are all included within the elements, then they must exist as well. Since the reason these people had for believing

in the reality of things was that they believed in the true existence
of the elements, it was therefore necessary for Nagarjuna to examine
the elements and demonstrate that they are not truly existent at all.

The first verse from this chapter reads:

> Space can in no way exist
> Prior to its defining characteristics.
> If space existed prior to its defining
>   characteristics,
> It would follow that space could exist
>   without defining characteristics.

When Nagarjuna analyzed the sources of consciousness, he refuted their existence from the perspective of the relationship between perceiving subjects and perceived objects. When he examined
the aggregates, he refuted their existence from the perspective of
the relationship between causes and results. Here, when he analyzes
the elements, it is from the perspective of the relationship between the defining characteristics of something, or the basis to
which a particular name is given, and the definiendum, that which
is defined by those characteristics, the name that is given to that
basis. This chapter will show that this relationship too cannot be a
truly existent one.

Here Nagarjuna examines space, which except for consciousness
is the subtlest element. *Space* is the name, the definiendum, that
which is defined. Space's defining characteristics are that it does not
obscure or obstruct, meaning that it is a complete absence of existence; it is thoroughly intangible. That is how space is defined.

If space and its defining characteristics truly existed, they would
have to exist either sequentially or simultaneously. If they existed
sequentially, then the first possibility would be that space, the definiendum, existed before the characteristics that define it. That would
be impossible, however, because how could the thing that is being
defined exist before there are any characteristics to define it? If it

did, then space would exist without its defining characteristics. There would be space without any qualities of unobstructedness or lack of obscuration.

It would also be impossible for the defining characteristics to exist before the definiendum did, for how could there be defining characteristics if there was nothing that they defined? Defining characteristics have to be the defining characteristics of something in order to exist, and therefore the defining characteristics cannot exist before the phenomenon that they define does.

Nor can the defining characteristics and the definiendum exist simultaneously. If they did, and they truly existed independently, then there would be no connection between them. They would be like a cow and a horse: They would be independent entities that would not have any relationship with each other. This is not how it is with the defining characteristics and the definiendum, however. There has to be some connection between them, because each one depends upon the other for its existence. If they existed simultaneously as independent entities, then they would not be dependent upon each other, and therefore each would exist without a cause.

We need to understand what it means to say that something truly exists. What characteristics would something need to have in order to be truly existent? It would have to exist independently, with its own inherent nature; it would have to exist without depending on anything else and be impervious to causes and conditions acting upon it. If it were like that, then we could say it was real.

However, for there to be characteristics of something depends upon there being something to have those characteristics, and vice versa; for there to be defining characteristics there must be a definiendum, and vice versa. In this case the characteristics of space exist in dependence upon there being some space to possess the characteristics; but also, the space can exist only when it has some characteristics to define it. Since each of them has to depend upon the other to exist, they have no nature of their own; they do not truly exist.

This is the logical reasoning that dispels any belief that space and its defining characteristics are truly existent. Does that mean, though, that they are completely nonexistent? No, it does not. There still is a dependently arisen appearance of space and of all of the elements, just like when they appear in dreams, just like the appearance of a water-moon. So we have no need to worry or be frightened, because the conclusion is not that the elements are completely nonexistent. It would be a big problem if space were nonexistent, because then we could not fly in airplanes! There is, in fact, a mere appearance of space that is the union of dependent arising and emptiness.

There are many reasonings in this chapter, but the verse that sums them all up is the seventh:

> Therefore, space is not something, it is not
>   nothing,
> It is not a basis for characteristics, its
>   defining characteristics do not exist,
> And the other five elements are precisely
>   the same.

We should examine all the other elements and their respective characteristics in the same way that we have examined space. This will be easy, because we apply the same analysis we have used before. It is just like when a new style of clothes comes out: Once someone has made the clothes in white, it is easy to copy the same pattern in red, blue, green, or any other color! So, in the same way that we have looked at space, we should look at earth and its characteristics of being hard and obstructing; fire and its characteristics of being hot and burning; water and its characteristics of being wet and moistening; wind and its characteristics of being light and moving; and consciousness and its characteristics of being clear and aware. By analyzing them in that way, we will see that none of them truly exists. In every case, it is impossible for either the defining characteristics or the definiendum to exist before the other; it is impossible for them to exist simultaneously; and there is no other alternative for how they could be. Therefore, they are all empty of their own essence; they all lack true existence.

At the level of thorough analysis, the true nature of space and its defining characteristics is found to be the freedom from all conceptual fabrications. We cannot say that they are something, because when we analyze we cannot find anything there; nor can we say that they are nothing, because there is the mere appearance of them that arises due to causes and conditions. Therefore, they are the union of appearance and emptiness, whose nature is beyond all of our concepts of what it might be. The same is true for all the other elements as well.

In the eighth and last verse in the chapter, Nagarjuna comments on this further:

> Those with little intelligence
> View things as being existent or
>   nonexistent.
> They do not see that what is to be seen
> Is perfect and utter peace.

When we do not have much understanding of reality, we either think that things exist, meaning that they are real, or we think they do not exist, that there is absolutely nothing, not even a mere appearance. These views of existence and nonexistence obscure our realization of the true nature of reality. The true nature of reality is peace, in the sense that no conceptual fabrication can accurately describe it. It cannot be said to be either existent or nonexistent. Within it, all conceptual fabrications are perfectly at peace.

If we put this in the form of a logical reasoning, we would say: Those with little intelligence do not see pure reality free from the fabrications of existence and nonexistence, because they think either that things exist or that they do not. They think either that there is something truly there or that there is nothing there at all. They do not realize that appearances are mere dependently arisen appearances, and so they cannot see the true nature of reality beyond fabrication.

On the other hand, those who have great intelligence are able to transcend the fabrications of existence and nonexistence and see pure reality. They do not have the view of existence—they do not think things are real—nor do they have the view of nonexistence, which would be to think that there is absolutely nothing. They perfectly understand the union of appearance and emptiness, of dependent arising and emptiness, and this frees them from extreme views. They would not even claim to abide in the "middle" in between the extremes, because if the extremes do not exist, how could there be any middle in between them?

As the Buddha said in the *King of Samadhi Sutra*:

> "Existence" and "nonexistence" are both
>   extremes,
> "Pure" and "impure" are the same.
> Therefore, abandoning all extremes,
> The wise do not even abide in the middle.

The wise are completely free from all concepts about the true nature of reality, including concepts of the extremes and even concepts of some middle ground in between the extremes.

6

An Examination of Desire and the Desirous One

In the *Sutra of the Great Mother*, the Buddha taught:

Desire is perfectly pure, and therefore forms are perfectly pure.

❈ ❈ ❈ ❈ ❈

THE BUDDHA EXPLAINED perfect purity in a vast way. The reason desire is perfectly pure is that desire and the one who experiences it do not truly exist; they are not real. Therefore, there is no flaw in having desire; there is no flaw in the desire itself because it has no inherent nature. Its nature is therefore said to be perfectly pure.

The desire itself is perfectly pure, and therefore the desirous one—the one who has the desire—is perfectly pure, and the object of desire is perfectly pure. In brief, that is the way it is.

If the essence of desire were in fact impure, then the desirous one would be impure and the object of the desire would be impure as well. However, since the essential nature of desire in a dream is perfectly pure, since it is free from any stain, the nature of the one who is feeling that desire is perfect purity without any stain, and the nature of the object of the desire is perfect purity free from stain. In the *Sutra of the Great Mother*, there is one chapter called *Perfect Purity*, comprising several volumes, and in one passage from this chapter the Buddha states, "Desire is perfectly pure, and therefore forms are perfectly pure. Forms are perfectly pure, and therefore transcendent generosity is perfectly pure. Transcendent generosity is perfectly pure, and therefore the omniscience of the Buddha is perfectly pure." It would be good for you to read the chapter called *Perfect Purity*, because it is easy to understand and those who read it like it very much.

The reason Nagarjuna composed this chapter examining desire and the desirous one was that even after he presented the analyses of the sources of consciousness, aggregates, and elements that demonstrate that none of these truly exist, those who asserted the true existence of things claimed that these things do in fact exist because the mental afflictions that arise in dependence upon them exist. For example, desire exists, and this proves that the objects that desire focuses upon exist as well, because desire could not exist in their absence. Since the reason they used to try to prove that things exist is that desire exists, it was necessary for Nagarjuna to analyze and refute the true existence of desire and the desirous one.

The Vajrayana explains that the mental afflictions—the five poisons of anger, desire, stupidity, pride, and jealousy—are all perfectly pure, and so this chapter that analyzes this very point is very important to Vajrayana practice. The analysis in this chapter is applicable to all of the mental afflictions. It starts out with desire, but it can then be applied to anger, pride, jealousy, and stupidity. The reason the focus is explicitly on desire is that we are all inhabitants of the desire realm, and all of the beings in the desire realm, from the tiniest insects up to the mightiest gods and goddesses, have a lot of desire.[11] That is why it is important for us to examine desire and determine that its nature is in fact perfectly pure.

Gendun Chöpel composed the following verse:

> Blind ants run in pursuit of happiness,
> Legless worms crawl in pursuit of
>   happiness,
> In short, all beings think nothing of
>   climbing over one another in their
>   pursuit of happiness—
> All beings strive only to be happy.

The crux of this is that all beings in the desire realm have a lot of desire, which is why it is essential for us to determine that desire is perfectly pure.

The first verse in this chapter that helps us determine the purity of desire and the desirous one reads:

> If before desire existed,
> If without any desire there existed a
>   desirous one,
> In dependence upon that, there would in
>   fact be desire,
> For when there is a desirous one, there is
>   also desire.

Here we are looking at the desirous one—which could refer either to the desirous individual or to the mind that experiences desire—and the desire itself. We can ask, if these things truly exist, how do

---

11. There are three realms inhabited by the sentient beings in samsara: the desire realm, the form realm, and the formless realm. The latter two are more subtle and are the exclusive domain of certain gods who have spent a long time cultivating specific meditative states of absorption. The desire realm is populated by all six classes of sentient beings: beings in the hell realms, hungry ghosts, animals, humans, and certain types of gods.

they exist in terms of their sequence? Does one happen before the other, or do they occur simultaneously? We cannot say that the desire exists before the desirous one, because if it did, there would be disembodied desire floating around out there without anyone to experience it, and that would not make any sense. On the other hand, it cannot be that the one who experiences the desire, the desirous being, exists before the desire itself, because if that were the case, then there would be a desirous individual without any desire. It would necessarily follow that arhats[12] and buddhas would be desirous individuals, because in order to fit the definition of a desirous individual, it would not matter if the being had desire or not. That would not make sense either. Neither can desire and the desirous one exist simultaneously, because if they came into existence at the same time, each with its own inherent nature, there would not be any connection between them. They would be two independent things, existing separately, that could each go its own separate way. One could cease and the other could still remain. That is clearly not the case with desire and the desirous one—they can exist only in mutual dependence. Since they cannot exist sequentially and they cannot exist simultaneously, desire and the desirous one are not real; they are just like appearances in a dream.

We need to apply the same reasoning to anger and the angry one, to jealousy and the jealous one, to pride and the proud one, and to stupidity and the stupid one. We can apply the same analysis to all of these, and we should. The Vajrayana instructs us to bring the five poisons to the path, and the reasons that is possible are explained here in this chapter—in fact there are no other reasons than these.

---

12. An arhat is one who has attained the highest fruition, the nirvana of either the Shravakayana or Pratyekabuddhayana (see note 16, page 60). By cultivating strong revulsion for and renunciation of samsara, and by perfecting their realization of the selflessness of the individual, the arhats completely free themselves from the mental afflictions and gain liberation from samsara. At a certain point, however, the buddhas wake them up from the peace of their meditative state, reveal to them that they have not yet attained the fruition of buddhahood itself, and exhort them to practice the Mahayana teachings for the benefit of all sentient beings. Doing so, they eventually attain the complete and perfect enlightenment of the buddhas.

We can look at anger and see that before the anger arises there is no angry person. It would be impossible for there to be an angry individual before the anger itself. For example, while someone is meditating on loving-kindness, there is no angry person, but if anger should arise later, there will be an angry person. So the angry person cannot exist before the anger itself. Nor can the anger exist before the one who is angry, nor can they exist simultaneously. Therefore, they cannot truly exist.

We can apply the same analysis to suffering. We need to examine suffering and the one who suffers to see which one comes first, and we see that whatever way we posit the relationship between them, it is logically impossible. Therefore, neither suffering nor the one who suffers is real.

We can look in the same way at sickness and the one who is sick: Which one comes first, the sick individual or the sickness itself? If the sick individual existed before the sickness itself, all healthy sentient beings would also be sick. In fact, sickness depends upon there being a sick individual, and vice versa, and therefore neither of them inherently exists. This is important for us to know. The great siddha Gotsangpa sang in his vajra song of realization called *The Eight Cases of Basic Goodness* that sickness is not to be shunned because it is basically good; mental afflictions are not to be shunned because they are basically good; and suffering is not to be shunned because it is basically good, and we need to know the reasons that this is true.[13]

The same can be applied to the expectations of difficulties in the future and the problems those expectations create for us. When we expect to experience difficulties in the future, we should examine which exists first—the one who is going to experience these problems or the future problems themselves? If the causes of future suffering do not exist, then the future suffering itself does not exist. If the future suffering itself does not exist, then the individual who

---

13. Gyalwa Gotsangpa was an emanation of Milarepa and a great early master of the Drukpa Kagyü lineage, four generations removed from Lord Gampopa, Milarepa's greatest disciple.

will suffer in the future cannot be said to exist either. Therefore, the true nature of future suffering is perfect purity, and the experience of the realization of that is open, spacious, and relaxed.

In this way, beginning with desire, we find that whatever we analyze, its nature is perfect purity. Furthermore, we can examine more and more things and see that they are all also perfectly pure by their very nature, and this allows us to experience more and more openness, spaciousness, and relaxation.

7

An Examination of
the Composite

In the sutras, the Buddha taught:

Considering the composite, the noncomposite, positive
actions, and negative ones,
When we examine them with precise knowledge, we find
not the slightest trace of their existence.

❀ ❀ ❀ ❀ ❀

WHEN WE EXAMINE THINGS and cannot find the slightest trace of
their existence, emptiness becomes easy to understand. To help us
in this endeavor, Nagarjuna proves the validity of this teaching of
the Buddha's with logical reasoning.

There were those who claimed that composite things are real because a composite thing is defined by its characteristics of arising,
abiding, and ceasing, and this arising, abiding, and ceasing are real.
Thus, to help these people understand that composite entities are
empty of their own essence, in this chapter Nagarjuna analyzes aris-

ing, abiding, and ceasing and demonstrates that they do not truly happen after all.

Some people ask, what would be the characteristics of something that truly existed? If something truly existed, it would exist on its own, by itself, objectively, without depending on anything else.

Here we are looking at arising, abiding, and ceasing. If these three truly existed, then arising would exist on its own without depending on any concept of ceasing. It would exist completely by itself. Abiding would also exist on its own, without depending on arising or ceasing. Finally, ceasing would exist independently, without needing any arising or abiding to occur. If it were really like that, then one could say that these things truly exist, that they have their own inherent nature. We can analyze, however, and see that each one of these three has to depend on the others for its existence. This is why the Middle Way explains that these things do not have their own nature, that they are empty of true existence.

This can be proven with logical reasoning in the following way: Arising does not inherently exist because it depends for its existence upon the cessation of its cause—if its cause does not cease, there can be no arising of any result, whatever it might be. Abiding does not inherently exist because it depends upon arising—abiding can occur only if something has arisen in the first place. Finally, cessation does not inherently exist because it can occur only if something has first arisen and then abided for some period of time. Thus, arising, abiding, and ceasing can exist only in mutual dependence—for one to exist the others must exist, but for those others to exist the first one must exist. They therefore do not truly exist; they are dependently arisen mere appearances.

Nagarjuna sums up the implications of this in the thirty-third verse:

> Arising, abiding, and ceasing do not exist,
> And therefore there are no composite
>   things.

> Since composite things are utterly
>   nonexistent,
> How could anything noncomposite exist?

The defining characteristics of a composite phenomenon are that it arises due to causes and conditions, then it abides, and then it ceases. The defining characteristics of a noncomposite phenomenon are that it does not arise, abide, or cease.[14]

If we put this verse in the form of a logical reasoning, we would say: Forms and so forth—all things that are composite—do not inherently exist because they do not arise, they do not abide, and they do not cease. It is accurate to say that there is no true arising, abiding, or ceasing because arising, abiding, and ceasing cannot exist inherently, but only in dependence upon each other.

Furthermore, noncomposite phenomena do not truly exist, because they depend for their existence upon composite phenomena, and composite phenomena themselves do not truly exist. Noncomposite phenomena do not arise, abide, or cease—they are the absence of arising, abiding, and ceasing. If these three activities do not exist in the first place, how could their absence exist?

In order to understand this better, think about a car in a dream. The car is the appearance of a composite phenomenon that arises, abides, and ceases, and the space inside the car is the opposite of that—it is a noncomposite phenomenon that neither arises, abides, nor ceases. If the dream car itself does not really exist, how could

---

14. There are three different noncomposite phenomena: space, the cessation that is the result of analysis, and the cessation that is not the result of analysis. The second refers to the absence of mental afflictions and suffering in the mindstream of an arhat who has realized the selflessness of the individual through analysis. The third refers to any cessation or absence of something that is not the result of the arhat's analysis; in other words, all the ordinary instances of the nonexistence or cessation of things that occur in the world on an everyday basis. For example, the nonexistence of elephants on the moon is an instance of this third type of noncomposite phenomena. All three of these share the common trait of being the absence of things that arise, abide, and cease. Noncomposite phenomena do not arise, abide, or cease because there is nothing there to arise, abide, or cease. They are the opposite of—the nonexistence of—things that do arise, abide, and cease.

the space inside the car really exist? Both are just dependently arisen mere appearances.

This is something Nagarjuna explains in verse thirty-four, the last verse of the chapter—how it is not illogical for arising, abiding, and ceasing to exist as dependently arisen mere appearances that have no inherent nature:

> Like a dream, like an illusion,
> Like a city of gandharvas,
> That's how birth and that's how living.
> That's how dying are taught to be.

Dreams, illusions, and cities of gandharvas are all examples of "empty forms"—things that appear without having any real existence—and these examples help us to understand how it could be possible for something to appear vividly at the same time that it is not real in the slightest way.

Gandharvas are a type of spirit. They live together in large communities, and when you look at them from far away it seems as if there is a whole city of them, but once you get close to them, they seem to vanish. They are a very good example of the big cities we live in these days—when we do not analyze, there seem to be a great many people there, but as soon as we look more closely, we cannot find any one of them that truly exists. Therefore, all those people are just mere appearances, like gandharvas.

In his *Guide to the Bodhisattva's Conduct*, the bodhisattva Shantideva teaches:

> Then wanderers, these dreamlike beings,
>   what are they?
> If analyzed, they're like a banana tree—
> One cannot make definitive distinctions
> Between transcending misery and not.

Sentient beings who wander in samsara are like sentient beings who appear in dreams. Once we analyze, we find that they are like banana trees—when you look at a banana tree, it seems solid, but once you peel away the layers of its bark, you do not find any core. The bodies of sentient beings are the same—they appear to be solid, truly existent things, but we can apply the analysis of composite entities that we have undertaken in this chapter to sentient beings' bodies as well and find that they are not truly existent after all, that they have no real substance, because they do not really arise, abide, or cease. Thus, sentient beings are illusory appearances.

In the Mahayana, the meditation that one practices in between formal meditation sessions is called the samadhi that sees everything to be like an illusion.[15] In the Vajrayana, this is called impure illusory body practice. The names are different, but the instructions for practicing them are the same: View all appearances of forms, sounds, smells, tastes, tactile sensations, and thoughts as appearing while empty, empty while appearing; understand all your experiences to be the union of appearance and emptiness, like illusions and dreams.

These days, the samadhi that sees everything to be like an illusion is easier to practice than ever before, because modern technology has produced so many new examples of empty forms. Movies, television, telephones, faxes, e-mail, the internet—all of these are wonderful examples of how things can appear due to the coming together of causes and conditions, while at the same time being empty of any inherent nature. In big cities, there are all kinds of flashing lights and moving billboards outdoors, and when you go into any big department store, there are huge mirrors on the walls, filled with reflected images. So the city is a wonderful place to train in the samadhi of illusion.

---

15. *Samadhi* refers to a state in which one is concentrated and not distracted. Paradoxically, it seems, the samadhi that sees everything to be like an illusion is the meditation one practices in the midst of all the distractions of thoughts and the objects that appear to the senses. When one remembers that all of these distractions are illusory, however, this constitutes the practice of this samadhi, and all the distractions are in fact friends of and enhancements to the meditation rather than hindrances or obstacles.

8

An Examination of Actors and Actions

In the *Sutras of the Mother*, the Buddha taught:

No actor is perceptible and no action is perceptible, either.

❁ ❁ ❁ ❁ ❁

IN THIS CHAPTER, Nagarjuna will prove the validity of this statement with logical reasoning.

Nagarjuna composed this chapter in answer to those who thought that composite things truly exist because the actors and actions that produce them truly exist. In order to demonstrate to these people that their belief was flawed, Nagarjuna had to examine actors and actions and demonstrate that they do not truly exist after all.

The way to analyze actors and actions is to examine the possible ways they could exist in relation to each other. If they do exist, do they exist sequentially or simultaneously? They cannot exist sequentially, because, first, the actor cannot exist before the action. If the actor did exist before and therefore independent of the action, then there would be a performer of an action even when the action was not being performed. For example, if the action was to write a letter and the actor was the letter writer, then there would be a letter writer who did not perform any action of writing a letter. Furthermore, the action cannot exist before and independent of the actor, for if it did, it would be an action without an actor performing it, which would be impossible. Since the actor can exist only if there is an action, but the action can exist only if there is an actor, they exist only in mutual dependence, and therefore they have no nature of their own. They do not truly exist.

Then one might ask, "I can see why the actor can't exist before the action and why the action can't exist before the actor, but why can't they exist at the same time?" The reason they cannot is that if they did, and each had its own inherent nature, there would not be any connection between them—they would be two independent things. To say that things exist inherently means that they do not exist in dependence upon each other. Here, though, the only reason we can say there is an actor is because there is some action, and the only reason we can say there is an action is because there is some actor. They have a relationship in which each is the cause of the other; they are dependent upon each other for their existence. This is why they cannot exist simultaneously as independent entities—if they did, they would not have that relationship of mutual dependence. Like a horse and a cow, each would be able to go its own way without any effect on the other at all.

We can put this in a form of a logical reasoning by saying: Neither an actor nor an action has any nature of its own, because for an actor to exist there must be an action, but that action can exist only in dependence upon the actor herself. Since they can exist only in mutual dependence, they do not truly exist.

Thus, actors and actions do not truly exist because they cannot exist independent of each other. They do, however, exist as dependently arisen mere appearances that manifest due to the coming together of causes and conditions. To explain this, Nagarjuna writes in verse twelve:

> An actor exists in dependence upon an
>   action,
> An action exists in dependence upon an
>   actor,
> And apart from that,
> No reason for their existence can be seen.

It is very good for us to know the root verses of this text, as opposed to merely receiving a general explanation of their meaning, because then we can be certain of what the text actually says. In fact the Sanskrit version of this text exists, as does the Tibetan translation, and now there are translations into English and other languages. If you like, you can compare these different versions in order to gain a better understanding of their meaning. To have at least one version to refer to helps us to have a good and stable understanding of what this text is about.

There are three ways of understanding actors and the karmic actions that they perform. When explanations are given to beginners about karma and the actors who perform karmic actions, these things are explained as if they really exist. We have to understand, though, that this is from the perspective of no analysis, the perspective of just taking appearances to be real, without analyzing them. The next step is to analyze with precise knowledge, and when we do that, then we see, as we have done here, that actors and actions are not real, that they do not really exist at all. The ultimate understanding is that the true nature of actors and actions is beyond any conceptual notion of them, whether it be a thought that they exist or that they do not exist. Their actual nature transcends both of those concepts, and this third stage presents the ultimate way to understand reality. It is important for us to distinguish these three stages of no analysis, slight analysis, and thorough analysis, because by doing so it becomes clear that there are no contradictions in the Buddha's teachings. At the same time, our respect for the Buddha's skill in presenting teachings of gradually increasing levels of subtlety and profundity will grow.

9

An Examination of What Comes First

In the sutras, the Buddha taught:

> Composite things are empty of the self of the individual and the self of phenomena.

And:

> Sentient beings do not exist, so no life force can be found
>   either—
> These phenomena are like bubbles of foam and banana trees,
> Like illusions, like lightning in the sky,
> Like water-moons, like mirages.

❖ ❖ ❖ ❖ ❖

THE WORDS IN THIS SECOND VERSE are beautiful—it would be very good if you memorized it.

In this chapter, Nagarjuna will explain these passages and prove their validity with logical reasoning. Nagarjuna composed this chap-

ter in answer to the members of the five out of the eighteen sub-
schools of the Shravakayana that claimed that the "self of the
individual," meaning the self of the individual sentient being, substantially exists.[16] Nagarjuna analyzes the self of the individual and
shows that it does not substantially exist, but rather is a mere appearance that manifests due to the coming together of causes and
conditions.

This chapter contains many logical reasonings that refute the
view that the self exists substantially. The twelfth and final verse
summarizes them all in the following way:

> The one who experiences perceptions does
>   not exist
> Before, during, or after the experiences of
>   seeing and so forth.
> Knowing this, all thoughts of an
>   experiencer of perceptions either
>   existing or not existing are reversed.

The one who sees form cannot exist before—that is, independent
of—the experience of seeing the form, for if she did, it would ab-
surdly follow that she would always see that form. The reason for
this is that if an individual is called a "seer of form," it is obviously
because she actually sees some form, and thus if the seer of form
existed independent of the experience of seeing it, the self who was
called the seer of form would always see the form in order to earn
that name. The same would be true with the other objects of the
senses and the ones who experience them—if the experiencer existed before the experience itself, it would follow that the experiencer would always have that experience. Thus, if the hearer of a

16. The Shravakayana (vehicle of the hearers) and the Pratyekabuddhayana (vehicle of the
solitary buddhas) compose the Hinayana, the foundational vehicle of Buddhism, whose views
and practices are based on the first turning of the wheel of Dharma.

particular sound existed before the hearing of it, then that individual would always hear that sound. If the smeller of a particular smell existed before experiencing the smell of it, then that individual would always smell the same smell. If the taster of a particular taste existed before tasting it, then that self would always taste the same taste. Finally, if the experiencer of bodily sensation existed before the feeling of it, then that individual would always experience that same sensation.

Therefore, no self can exist before the perceptions of forms, sounds, smells, tastes, and tactile sensations it experiences, because if it did, and it were one self, then it would be the seer of form before it saw anything, the hearer of sound before it heard anything, the smeller of odors before it smelled anything, and so forth. It would be having all of the future experiences at once because it would be the experiencer of all those experiences before it experienced them. If it so happened that the experiencers of the different perceptions were different from each other, then if all of those existed before the experiences themselves, there would be that many selves existing at the same time in one individual, which would be illogical.

Furthermore, if the self who sees something existed after the experience of seeing ceased, there would be a self who sees without any seeing occurring, which would also be logically impossible. Finally, if the self who experienced perception existed only at the same time as the sense perception and not before or after it, that self would just all of a sudden come into existence at that moment of perception and then would cease to exist once that moment was over.

Someone might say, "Even if the experiencer of any particular perception does not exist before the experience of it, but rather at the same time it occurs, it does not mean that the self who is the experiencer just came into being at that very moment, because in one moment the self may be the experiencer of form, then in the next moment the experiencer of sound, and so forth."

The question then becomes, is the self who is the hearer of a sound in one moment the same as or different from the self who is the seer of a form in the next moment? If it were the same self in both moments, meaning that the self with all its qualities were the same from moment to moment, then again there would be the logical flaw that the self who had the quality of being the one that saw a form would exist before that experience of seeing that form occurred. On the other hand, if the selves in each moment were different from each other, then in each moment there would be a completely different self who would instantaneously arise and cease and would have no connection with any of the selves that came before or after it. This, however, would totally contradict our notion of the self as continuing its existence over the entire period of this life, not to mention past and future lives. Therefore, this argument is also illogical.

Thus, the self cannot truly exist before, during, or after the experience of perceptions; but then, what is the self who appears to experience things? It is a dependently arisen mere appearance, just like the self who appears to experience things in dreams. When we analyze this self we cannot find it, so we cannot say that it exists, and since there is a mere appearance of it, we cannot say that it is completely nonexistent either. Therefore, the true nature of the self is appearance and emptiness inseparable, beyond the fabrications of existence, nonexistence, and whatever else we might think it to be.

We should apply this line of reasoning to other aspects of our existence as well. For example, we need to ask, does the one who gives rise to faith exist before the faith itself, or not? Does the one who has wrong views exist before the wrong views, or not? If the self does exist before those experiences, is it one self or different selves? Examine this and see.

We can also apply this analysis to the life of someone like the great Dharma king Ashoka, who first did a lot of negative things and later did a lot of positive things. Did the one who performed positive actions and the one who acted negatively exist before those specific actions themselves? If the one who acted positively and the one who acted negatively did exist before those actions, did they exist at the same time, in the same individual as different selves? How did they exist?

If someone is going to go for refuge, we can ask the question, does the one who goes for refuge exist before the act of going for refuge, or not? If she does so exist, then do the self who goes for refuge and the self who has not gone for refuge exist at the same time, or not?

This is a very profound and subtle way to analyze, and it is also an easy way to analyze, so we should use it a lot! We can apply it to a worldly situation, to someone who is out of work and then gets work. There is the self who is out of work and then the self who gets work—are they the same self? Are the out-of-work self and the working self the same, or are they different? Does the out-of-work self exist at the same time as the working self, and if so, are they one and the same, or are they different selves existing at the same time? Or are they different selves existing at different times?

When we analyze in this way, we can come to an extraordinary certainty in the emptiness of the self of the individual and in the union of appearance and emptiness that is beyond conceptual fabrication. To put this into verse for you:

> When you think, "I exist" or "I don't
>   exist,"
> That's how you fall into realism or become
>   a nihilist.
> To know your true nature, think of a clear
>   sky at night
> And on a beautiful lake, a moon that shines
>   so bright!
> Appearance and emptiness, no one can
>   separate—
> This is how you have to meditate!

10

An Examination of Fire and Firewood

In the sutras, the Buddha explained:

When one's hands, two sticks, and one's effort of rubbing the sticks come together,
From these conditions, fire arises,
And after arising and performing its function, it quickly ceases.
But when the wise ones ask,
"Where did it come from and where did it go?"
They look in all directions, but never find any occurrence of its coming or going.

So it is with the aggregates, sources of consciousness, and potentials—
They do not exist inside and they do not exist outside;
All are free of self-entity,
And they do not abide anywhere.
The defining characteristic of phenomena is that they are of the essence of space.

❖ ❖ ❖ ❖ ❖

WHEN OUR HANDS rub two sticks together, that produces a fire that will eventually cease, but this fire does not come from anywhere to the sticks when it first begins to burn them and it does not go anywhere when it goes out. Fire is empty of coming and going.

Similarly, ignorance, clinging to the belief in self, mental afflictions, and suffering do not come from anywhere and they do not go anywhere. We can apply this to the experience of dreams as well and see that whatever appears in dreams, whatever happiness or suffering, it does not come from anywhere and it does not go anywhere. In the very same way, all phenomena are empty of coming and going.

Nagarjuna composed this chapter in answer to those who did not accept his refutation of the self of the individual from the last chapter. These people claimed that the self exists in relation to the five aggregates in the same way that fire exists in relation to the wood that it burns. Just as the fire is the burning agent and firewood is the object burned, so it is that the self is the appropriator and the aggregates are the objects that it appropriates. In order to help these people abandon their belief that the self was real, Nagarjuna therefore had to examine fire and firewood and demonstrate that they do not truly exist.

One way that Nagarjuna does this is by showing that two things like fire and firewood[17] that must depend upon each other for their existence cannot truly exist. This is the topic of verse ten:

> If something exists in dependence upon
>   something else,
> But that thing upon which it depends
> Must also depend upon it,
> Then which one of these exists in
>   dependence upon which?

---

17. The term *firewood* here means wood that is actually being consumed by fire.

If fire and the wood that it burns truly exist, they have to exist either independently or dependently—there is no third alternative. The fire and the wood that it burns cannot exist independent of each other, however, because if they could, then fire could exist even in the absence of anything to burn, and burning wood could exist without any fire burning it. So the first possibility is eliminated.

The fire and firewood cannot actually exist dependently either. If they did, then one of the two would have to first exist and then serve as a cause to bring the other into existence. Neither fire nor the wood that it burns can fulfill that function, however, because each depends upon the other for its own existence. Fire can exist only if there is something burning, but that burning substance (the firewood) cannot exist unless there is some fire burning it! So even though the fire relies on the burning wood for its existence, the burning wood itself cannot exist first and then bring the fire into existence, because for it to exist there must be a fire burning it in the first place. Similarly, the fire cannot first exist and then serve as a supporting cause to bring the burning wood into existence, because the fire itself cannot exist unless there is some wood burning in the first place. In his commentary, Mipham Rinpoche gives the example of two rocking boats—since neither boat is steady to begin with, it is impossible for either one to be the cause of steadying the other. Similarly, when one thing must depend upon another for its existence, but that other one must in turn depend on the first for its own existence, in genuine reality it is impossible for either one to be the support for the other's existence. Therefore, neither one of them truly exists—they are mere interdependent appearances.

Another way to prove that fire and firewood lack inherent existence is to examine the five possible ways that fire and firewood could exist in relation to one another, and see that in fact none of them are possible. This is what Nagarjuna does in verse fourteen:

> The firewood itself is not the fire,
> There is no fire that exists apart from the
>   firewood,

The fire does not possess the firewood,
The fire does not support the firewood, and
    the firewood does not support the fire.

The first possibility is that fire and the firewood it burns would be the same thing. This would be illogical, however, because actors and the objects of their actions are not the same thing. For example, an ax is not the same thing as the wood it chops, a pen is not the same thing as the letters it writes, and so forth.

Second, it is impossible for the fire and the firewood to be different things, because if they were, they would exist independent of each other. Fire could burn in the sky without burning anything at all, and wood would burn without any fire burning it.

The last three possibilities—that the fire possesses the firewood, that the fire supports the firewood, or that the firewood supports the fire—all depend upon the fire and firewood being different entities, because there have to be two different things in order for one to possess or support the other. Since fire and firewood cannot be different entities, however, these last three possibilities are also impossible.

Thus, all five relationships that fire and firewood could possibly have with each other are logically untenable, and therefore, fire and firewood do not truly exist.

The next step is to apply this analysis to the self, the appropriator, and the five aggregates that it appropriates. Then we can apply it to all other phenomena as well. Nagarjuna does this in verse fifteen:

This examination of fire and firewood
Refutes the self and the aggregates it
    appropriates in all five ways.
Similarly, examining vases, blankets, and so
    forth,
It is perfectly explained that none of them
    exist in any of these five ways.

Just as fire and firewood cannot exist in relation to each other in any of the five possible ways, the same is true for the self and the aggregates it appropriates. The self is not the same as the aggregates, because it would be illogical for the appropriator and the objects it appropriates to be the same thing. Nor can the self be different from its aggregates, because the self cannot exist apart from the aggregates, which compose its body and mind, and these aggregates cannot exist apart from the self, for if they did they would be a body and mind that did not belong to anyone. The remaining three possibilities are all variants of the second one, so they too are logically untenable.[18]

If we go through the five possibilities one by one with regard to the aggregate of forms, we would say:

> The self is not forms,
> The self is not something different from
> forms,
> The self does not have or possess any
> forms,
> The self does not exist in dependence upon
> forms,
> And forms do not exist in dependence
> upon the self.

If we connect this with the other four aggregates of feelings, discriminations, formations, and consciousnesses, then we have twenty-five different ways to analyze the selflessness of the individual. It would be very good for you to go through them on your own.

We should also apply the same analysis to vases, blankets, our own bodies, our possessions, friends, enemies, causes, results, and

---

18. For further explanation of why the self does not truly exist because it cannot exist as the same as or different from the five aggregates, see the first verse of chapter 18, "An Examination of Self and Phenomena."

so forth. Whatever it is, it does not truly exist because it cannot exist in relation to the parts that compose it in any one of these five possible ways. Therefore, all composite things are only dependently existent mere appearances—just like fire and firewood, just like the self and the aggregates that compose it. All phenomena are therefore empty of self-nature—their defining characteristic is that they are of the essence of space.

What is it like for yogis and yoginis who directly realize this? Their realization brings them incredible power and freedom, as the Buddha taught in the *King of Samadhi Sutra*:

> Fire can blaze hot for hundreds of aeons
> But it will never be able to burn space.
> Similarly, fire will never be able to burn
> Those who know that phenomena are
>   equivalent to space.

When you dream and you know that you are dreaming, harmful things may appear, but they will not harm you. You can sit in the middle of a rushing river or in the middle of a blazing fire and not get hurt in the slightest way. Yogis and yoginis who directly realize the union of appearance and emptiness have this same experience during the day—the biographies of the great siddhas are filled with stories of how they performed such miraculous feats for the benefit of others. That they had such power was a direct result of their realization of emptiness, and the first step toward achieving that direct realization is to gain certainty in emptiness using our intelligence, our power of analysis. The reasonings Nagarjuna presents in his *Fundamental Wisdom of the Middle Way* help us to do that, and that is why they are so important.

11

An Examination of Samsara

In the *Prajñāpāramitā Sutras*, the Buddha taught:
No beginning is perceptible,
No end is perceptible,
And nothing in between is perceptible either.

❊ ❊ ❊ ❊ ❊

THE REASON THE WORD *perceptible* is used here is that if we examine with our eye of wisdom, we cannot perceive any earlier, middle, or later period of time in samsara, because these things do not inherently exist. Even the buddhas in all their wisdom never perceived any earlier, middle, or later period of time, because there have never been any of these three times to perceive.

Nagarjuna composed this chapter because those who believed in the true existence of things said to him, "Follower of the Middle Way, you may have attempted to refute the true existence of the self of the individual with your clever examples of fire and firewood, but you have not succeeded in doing so, because samsara exists. Since samsara exists, there must be someone to go around in samsara, and therefore the self does exist after all. Furthermore, since the self exists, the sources of consciousness, aggregates, and potentials that compose the self must also exist." Thus, Nagarjuna had to prove to these people that samsara does not truly exist, because if he had not done so, he would not have been able to help them overcome their confused belief in the true existence of the self.

If samsara actually existed, it would have to have a beginning, an end, and some span of time in the middle. Analysis, however, cannot find any beginning to samsara. Whatever our current situation in samsara, it had to have its own causes, and those causes had to have their own causes, and so on—nothing in the cycle of existence occurs without causes to bring it into being. We can therefore never find an "original cause" that would constitute the beginning of cyclic existence, because if there were one, it would have arisen without a cause itself, which is impossible. Thus, there was no point when samsara began, and how could something that never began ever end? Without a beginning or an end, how could there be any period of time in the middle? Since it has neither beginning, middle, nor end, samsara does not truly exist.

Another way to analyze samsara is to look at the relationship between samsara and the ones who supposedly wander around within it. Which of these comes first? If samsara existed before the ones who wander within it, there would be a samsara with nobody there. If the ones in samsara existed before samsara itself did, then where would they be? There would be nowhere for them to exist.

On the other hand, if samsara and the ones who wander in samsara existed simultaneously and they were inherently existent, they would have no connection with each other. They would each be able to go their own separate way independent of the other. It is not like that with respect to samsara and the beings within it, however.

They cannot exist independently or separately because each needs and depends upon the other to exist.

Once we discover that samsara does not truly exist, we find out what samsara actually is: a mistake. Samsara is not really there; it is just a mistake that we make, and nirvana is simply the correction of that mistake. We could also say that samsara is similar to dreaming and not knowing it is a dream—it is simply a misperception or mistaken understanding of the events that appear to be happening. Nirvana, in contrast, is like recognizing the dream for what it is.

In this chapter Nagarjuna also analyzes birth and death, and, by logically demonstrating that neither one of them actually takes place, he proves that the cycle of repeated births and deaths that constitutes samsara actually does not occur. In the chapter there is both a brief and an extensive explanation of this point, the former being given in the sixth verse:

> Since one cannot happen before the others,
> And they cannot happen simultaneously,
> Why would you ever think
> That birth, aging, and death truly exist?

If we put this verse in the form of a logical reasoning, we would say: As for birth, aging, and death, they have no nature of their own, they do not truly exist, because one cannot happen before the others and they cannot occur simultaneously. They cannot occur sequentially because, first of all, birth cannot precede death. This is the case because the arising of one moment cannot occur before the cessation of the previous moment. Death cannot precede birth either, because if it did there would be death without anything having been born. They cannot occur simultaneously either, for they are opposites—how can one thing arise and cease at the same time?

Here we are not considering the coarse level of appearances, for example, a baby being born and then growing old and dying. Rather, we must look at the more subtle level of existence of any particular thing, at how it arises and ceases instant by instant. For example, snap your fingers and see if you can distinguish between the arising and the cessation of that finger snap.

When did it arise? When did it cease? Even that finger snap is an incredibly coarse entity, and its arising and ceasing are equally coarse events. If we think about how many hundreds, thousands, and millions of subtle instants that arise and cease are included within the finger snap, then we start to realize that we cannot authentically distinguish between arising and ceasing. These events do not exist as independent, identifiable entities. Their existence is not perceptible to the eye of wisdom.

Birth, aging, and death are therefore like appearances in dreams. They are dependently arisen mere appearances that have no true existence. At the end of the verse, Nagarjuna asks, "Why would you ever think that birth, aging, and death truly exist?" There is not a single reason that can prove that birth, aging, and death are real, and there are so many reasons that prove that they are not real, so why would anyone who knew that continue to think of them as being truly existent?

What is the benefit of thinking that birth and death are real? How does that help? It only results in suffering. For example, when we dream, to believe that the birth, aging, and death that appear in the dream are real is not only unnecessary but harmful because it results in suffering. That is why it is so important to apply these reasonings and gain certainty that birth and death in samsara do not really exist, that they are just mere appearances that are like appearances in dreams and illusions.

Then you will see that samsara is just the erroneous belief that suffering is real, the erroneous belief that birth and death are real. Once we are free from the thought that suffering is real, we are no longer in samsara. Once we are free from the thought that birth and death are real, we will no longer be in samsara. In fact, since suffering, birth, and death do not really exist in the first place, samsara is just a mistake, just our making the mistake of thinking something is there that really is not there at all. Once we stop making that mistake, we are in nirvana.

That samsara is just a mistake and nirvana is when you simply stop making that mistake is the reason samsara and nirvana are actually undifferentiable, why they are of the nature of equality. The example of the dream makes this point clear. When you dream and do not know you are dreaming, the ignorance of the fact that it is a dream leads to attachment to some dream appearances and aversion to others, and this causes suffering. Once you realize that it is a dream, attachment and aversion dissolve and everything becomes open, spacious, and relaxed. From the perspective of the dream appearances themselves, however, nothing has changed at all. There was nothing wrong with those appearances in the first place, and therefore there were no flaws within them that needed to be abandoned or corrected, nor any positive qualities that needed to be added to them to make them better. They were originally pure and originally free, meaning that in their nature they transcended the characterizations of both confusion and realization, both suffering and bliss. Since from their own perspective there was never any confusion to begin with, there could be no liberation from confusion either. Since there was never any suffering inherent in them in the first place, they transcend the notion of the bliss that is the freedom from that suffering as well. In this way, the example of dream appearances illuminates the equality of ignorance and realization, of samsara and nirvana.

12

An Examination
of Suffering

In the *Prajñāpāramitā Sutras*, the Buddha taught:

Suffering is empty of suffering.

❄ ❄ ❄ ❄ ❄

THIS PARTICULAR TEACHING of the Buddha is a good example of teachings from the perspective of the *Rang-tong*, or "empty of self," school:[19] Whatever phenomenon it is, it is empty of its own essence; it is empty of what it appears to be; it is empty of itself. In this chapter, Nagarjuna proves the validity of this teaching with logical reasoning.

Nagarjuna composed this chapter in answer to those who believed that the self exists because suffering exists. Since there is suf-

---

19. The Rang-tong school is the branch of the Middle Way that bases its view on the second turning of the wheel of Dharma. It is composed of the Middle Way Autonomy and Middle Way Consequence schools.

fering, there has to be someone to experience the suffering, these people claimed. If Nagarjuna did not then prove to them that suffering was not real, it would have been impossible for him to help them see that there really is no self. That is why he analyzes suffering in this chapter and proves that it does not truly exist.

We can formulate many logical reasonings that prove that suffering is not real. For example: Suffering does not truly exist because there is not really anyone there to suffer—the self who supposedly suffers does not truly exist. Therefore, the suffering itself has no existent essence, and, just like in a dream, suffering is just our imagination. Isn't that good?

Furthermore, suffering does not truly exist because it does not come from anywhere and it does not go anywhere, and because it does not arise and it does not cease.

And further, suffering does not truly exist because the one who suffers, namely, the self, and the suffering that the self experiences cannot be the same thing and they cannot be different things. If they were the same thing, then the one who suffers would always be suffering. If they were different things, they would exist in different places with no connection between them. Therefore, they cannot be the same and they cannot be different, and since there is no other possibility for how they could be, they cannot truly exist.

What's more, suffering does not truly exist because the causal conditions that bring it about do not truly exist, as is the case with future suffering, for example. The causes of future suffering do not exist because they are in the future, and since they do not exist, future suffering that is their result does not exist, either.

When we know that suffering does not truly exist, it becomes clear that suffering in apparent reality is the mere lack of knowledge that suffering is not real. It is the mistaken belief that suffering is real when in fact it is not. It is like when we dream and do not know that we are dreaming.

If suffering were real, if it objectively existed, it would have to display some signs of that. There are no signs of its true existence, however, because suffering does not exist inherently or independently. Rather, it only appears to exist when certain causes and conditions come together. What is more, suffering cannot exist apart from any thought of it—it must depend upon the thought of the suffering in order to exist. Without the concept of suffering, there is no suffering in the slightest. Since it cannot exist on its own, it cannot have any objective or true existence.

The fact that suffering is just a thought and nothing else is something we definitely know from our own experience. For example, people can be very upset before they go to sleep, but when they are in deep sleep they do not suffer at all, because they do not have the thought of suffering. Then when they wake up again in the morning, they do not suffer at all until they start thinking of their suffering. Once they start thinking of it, then it begins, but not before.

If we examine in this way, we will understand what characteristics suffering would have to have if it were real, and we will understand that since it does not have those characteristics, it is not real.

Verse ten of this chapter explains how the analysis of suffering can be applied to everything else as well:

> That which is only suffering does not arise
> From any of the four extremes, and not
>   only that,
> All outer phenomena do not arise
> From any of the four extremes either.

"That which is only suffering" refers to the five aggregates that constitute the individual. In the Shravaka tradition, these are taught to be "only suffering" because they are both the result of defiled karmic action and the basis for the arising of the mental afflictions, which are suffering in and of themselves as well as being the cause of further karmic actions that produce even more suffering in the future. This is why the goal of the Shravakayana is to abandon the five aggregates and attain the state of nirvana, where not even the slightest trace of them remains. The nirvana of the Shravaka tradition is described as being like when a candle flame goes out—it is the peace that is the complete cessation of the defiled aggregates and samsara as well.

The Mahayana does not present things in this way, however. The Buddha taught many times in the Mahayana sutras that the five aggregates, and the suffering that goes along with them, are of the nature of original and perfect purity. There is not the tiniest bit of impurity anywhere within them that needs to be abandoned. Therefore, Mahayana practitioners do not want to be rid of their samsaric existence, but rather they aspire to take birth in samsara in as many bodies, in as many lifetimes as possible to be of benefit to sentient beings. In Vajrayana practice, one cultivates the understanding that the five aggregates are of the nature of the five buddha families and that suffering is of the nature of bliss. Since that is the case, why would one ever want to abandon them? They are of the very essence of enlightenment.

The key to understanding the Mahayana and Vajrayana views lies in Nagarjuna's reasonings. This is because the reason the aggregates and suffering can be described as being pure by nature is that they are empty by nature—they are unborn. They never actually come into existence. Something that never really comes into existence cannot possibly be impure, for what is there to be impure in the first place? It is like getting covered with filth in a dream—no matter how dirty you might seem to be, since not a single particle of the filth is real, in fact there is no impurity at all. Since there is no impurity, there cannot actually be any purity either, just as when you take a bath in the dream after having gotten so filthy, your cleanliness after the bath is just as lacking in reality as the dirtiness that preceded it. Therefore, the true nature of the dream transcends both purity and impurity, and this is given the name "original purity." We have to understand that what original purity refers to is the freedom from all fabrications, the emptiness in which we can gain certainty by using Nagarjuna's reasonings.

If we now examine suffering in the way that is described in this verse, we can determine that it is of the nature of emptiness because it does not arise from any of the four extremes. The first of these extremes would be to think that suffering came from itself, that suffering produced itself. If it did that, however, then it would have to exist first and then bring itself into existence once more. It would have to exist and then it would arise. That is obviously not what happens, however, because we can be incredibly happy and then all of a sudden great suffering can occur—the suffering can arise very quickly where it did not exist before in any way. So the suffering does not produce itself because it occurs anew.

Suffering does not arise from a cause that is different from itself either, because "difference" implies that there are two things simultaneously existent to compare with each other. At the time that the suffering itself exists, however, the causal conditions that bring it into existence do not exist, and thus there is no cause existent for the suffering to be different from. As we learned in chapter 1, cause and result do not exist simultaneously: When the cause exists the result does not, and when the result exists the cause does not, as is the case with a seed and its sprout. Therefore, results cannot arise from things that are different from themselves, because at the time they exist, there are no causes for the results to be different from; and therefore, suffering does not arise from something different from itself, because there is nothing for it to be different from.

The third possibility is that suffering would come from both itself and something other than itself. That is impossible, however, because all of the flaws in saying that suffering comes from itself and all the flaws of saying that it comes from something other than itself accrue to this third alternative.

The fourth extreme is to believe that suffering occurs without any cause at all. That is also impossible, because nothing can arise without causes and conditions. Whatever we perceive in the world, whatever suffering we experience, we know that it does not appear without causes and conditions.

Therefore, suffering does not really happen after all because it does not arise from any of the four extremes, and there are no other possibilities. All outer things are the same—they actually do not arise because they do not arise from any of the four extremes.

When you snap your fingers, that finger snap does not come from itself, does not come from something different from itself, does not come from both itself and something different from itself, and does not arise without any cause at all.

The same is true for all the thoughts that appear in the mind. Whether they are good or bad, profound or base, these thoughts do not come from themselves, do not come from something other than themselves, do not come from both themselves and something other than themselves, and do not arise without any cause at all. Rather, they are dependently arisen mere appearances, just like thoughts in a dream.

If thoughts were real, they would have to arise. If they arose, they would have to arise from one of these four possibilities. Since they do not arise from any one of these four possibilities, and these four are all the possibilities there are, thoughts do not truly arise, and therefore thoughts are not real.

Suffering does not ever really happen because it does not arise from any one of the four extremes. Nevertheless, there is the thought that thinks that suffering is real. Since this thought that thinks suffering is real does not arise from any one of the four extremes either, it is said to be self-liberated—its true nature is freedom.

13

An Examination of the Precise Nature of Reality

In the sutras, the Buddha said:

> Bhikshus, there is only one authentic undeceiving reality,
>   and that is the reality of nirvana.
> All composite things are deceptive and false.

❀ ❀ ❀ ❀ ❀

READING THIS TEACHING, we come to understand the importance of knowing the difference between apparent reality and genuine reality, between the way things appear and the way they really are. It is the case that even though things have no inherent nature because they do not arise from any of the four extremes, they still appear to arise to ordinary beings who, with their eyes of wisdom clouded by the cataracts of ignorance, believe this arising to be real. In this way, ordinary beings are like people who are tricked by a magician's illusions into thinking that the illusory animals that the magician has conjured up are real. To use a modern example, they are like children watching a movie, who get frightened by the fierce lions and tigers they see on the screen because they do not know that the movie is not real.

On the other hand, noble buddhas and bodhisattvas who have directly realized the true nature of reality know that the appearances of phenomena arising, abiding, and ceasing are just mere appearances that have no inherent nature. They are like the adults watching the movie, who reassure the children that nothing on the screen can actually hurt them in any way because none of it is real. By teaching the children in this way, the adults impart to the children the knowledge they need so that they too can be unafraid. This is a good analogy for what the buddhas and bodhisattvas do for ordinary individuals who take up the path of Dharma.

Therefore, even though it is the case that all phenomena are of the nature of emptiness, it is nevertheless important for us to be able to distinguish between the way of appearance and the way of reality, because it is as a result of not knowing the way of reality that we ordinary beings mistakenly think that appearances are real, and that is what causes all our problems.

The dream is also a good example to refer to here. The difference between how we regard appearances when we know we are dreaming and how we regard them when we do not is similar to the difference between the way noble beings who have realized emptiness, and ordinary beings who have not done so, relate to the appearances they perceive.

As the glorious Chandrakirti states in his text *Entering the Middle Way*:

> There are two ways of seeing every thing,
> The perfect way and the false way,

So each and every thing that can ever be
   found
Holds two natures within.

And what does perfect seeing see?
It sees the suchness of all things.
And false seeing sees what appears, no
      more—
This is what the perfect Buddha said.

The Mahayana practice of the samadhi that sees everything to be like an illusion, the Vajrayana illusory body practice, and the Dzogchen practices of *korde rüshin* all have as their purpose the dissolution of thoughts that cling to appearances as being real.[20]

That is a description of the first reason Nagarjuna composed this chapter: to help us to distinguish between the mode of appearance and the mode of genuine reality, and thereby to stop thinking that they are the same thing—to stop mistaking the way things appear for the way things really are.

Even while accepting this distinction, however, there were those who claimed that apparent reality must have some true existence to it because genuine reality truly exists as "authentic undeceiving reality," as the Buddha taught. If there is genuine reality, they claimed, if there is emptiness that is the nature of apparent phenomena, then those apparent phenomena that have that emptiness as their nature must also exist. Otherwise, emptiness would have nothing to be the nature of, and therefore it could not exist either. This was their argument.

Therefore, the second reason Nagarjuna composed this chapter was to examine emptiness and demonstrate that in fact it does not

20. Dzogchen, like Mahamudra, is a set of teachings that describes the true nature of reality and how to meditate upon it. *Korde rüshin* is one of the Dzogchen practices.

truly exist after all. This effectively refutes the claim that apparent
things truly exist because emptiness truly exists.

Nagarjuna takes up the analysis of emptiness in verse seven:

> If there were the slightest thing not empty,
> There would be that much emptiness
>   existent.
> Since, however, there is not the slightest
>   thing not empty,
> How could emptiness exist?

We can put this verse in the form of a logical reasoning in the
following way: Given the true nature of reality, emptiness does not
exist anywhere within it, because if there were something that was
not empty, there would be that much emptiness as well, but in fact
there is not the slightest thing that is not empty. Since there is not
the slightest thing not empty, there can be no emptiness either, because emptiness can exist only in dependence upon there being
something that is not empty, and something that is not empty can
only exist if there is emptiness. These two notions of *empty* and *not
empty* exist only in dependence upon each other, which means that
neither one of them truly exists. Therefore, neither the conceptual
fabrication of *empty* nor that of *not empty* applies to genuine reality.
Therefore, in order to realize the nature of essential reality beyond
conceptual fabrication, we must leave behind even our notion of
emptiness. This will also be explained in chapter 22, "An Examination of the Tathagatha."

14

An Examination
of Contact

In the *Sutra Requested by the Bodhisattva "Shining Intelligence,"* the
Buddha taught:

> Forms neither meet nor part.

✢ ✢ ✢ ✢ ✢

THIS TEACHING IS EASY to understand if we think of appearances
in dreams. Since the things that appear in dreams never truly meet,
they never truly part either. Even so, meeting and parting still appear to happen and we conceive of them as being real, and therefore
we must train in understanding their true nature. To put this into
verse for you:

> In this great expanse of space, without
>   center or end,

> On this planet, where there is neither top
>   nor bottom,
> Friends and enemies, it seems,
> Are forever meeting and parting,
> But please know that it is all just like a
>   dream!

Please do not take meeting and parting to be real.

Nagarjuna composed this chapter in answer to those who asserted that things do essentially exist because meeting and parting
exist. Meeting and parting occur all the time, they claimed, and
therefore there must be something to meet and part! However, the
mere appearance of meeting and parting and the corresponding
thought that they are real are not enough to establish their true
existence, because these appearances and thoughts also occur in
dreams. Therefore, in order to help these people understand that
things do not truly exist, Nagarjuna had to demonstrate logically
that meeting and parting are not real.

Nagarjuna analyzes meeting, or contact, with regard to sense perception. If sense perception truly occurred, there would have to be
some contact between the perceived object, the sense faculty, and
the perceiving sense consciousness. Thus the question is, is there
any contact between these three or not? Nagarjuna gives the answer
in the first verse of the chapter:

> The object seen, the eye that sees, and the
>   seer—
> These three do not meet each other,
> Either in pairs or all together.

Three things must come together in order for there to be a moment of eye sense perception: the object that is seen, the eye sense
faculty that sees, and the seer—the eye sense consciousness. "These
three do not meet each other in pairs" means that the eye does

not come into contact with the object that it sees; the eye sense consciousness does not come into contact with the object; and the eye sense consciousness does not come into contact with the eye. Therefore, they do not meet in pairs, nor do they all three meet together at the same time.

The reason the eye sense consciousness and the form that it perceives cannot meet each other is that the form is one of the causes of the eye sense consciousness—it is called the eye consciousness' focal condition. Therefore, the form that is the cause and the consciousness perceiving the form that is the result cannot exist at the same time, because if they did, one could not be the cause of the other. If the object perceived and the consciousness perceiving it come into existence simultaneously, then the former could not cause the latter to arise, because it would have no opportunity to do so. Logically, then, the form would have to occur before the eye sense consciousness if it were going to be its cause. It would have to cease before the eye sense consciousness arose, and that is why the two cannot meet.

Of course, this second possibility—that the perceived form precedes the sense consciousness that perceives it—is also impossible. If that were the case, the perceived object and the perceiving subject would be unable to make any connection with each other. If the perceived object ceased before the consciousness that perceived it arose, what precisely would that consciousness perceive? Its object would no longer exist! It would have nothing to perceive at all.

Since the perceived object and perceiving subject do not occur simultaneously or sequentially, sense perception is a mere appearance that does not truly exist.

The "self-liberation of contact through recollection" is an important Mahamudra practice in which one recalls again and again that the apparent meeting of consciousness and object is not a real occurrence; it is a mere appearance, the union of appearance and emptiness. The five sense consciousnesses are nonconceptual—they are free from any thoughts that things truly exist. The conceptual aspect of the mental consciousness, however, follows this direct valid cognition of the sense consciousnesses and conceives of the sense consciousnesses' experiences as being real. By following this thought of sense perception as being real with the recollection that the sense perception is appearance-emptiness, one practices self-liberation of contact through recollection, the remedy for that mistaken belief in the sense perceptions' true existence. Milarepa sang of this practice in several of his songs. It is an important practice because we have to realize the transcendence of the meeting of object, faculty, and consciousness if we are to realize the genuine nature of reality. If we still believe that the meeting of object, faculty, and consciousness is real, it is a sign that our certainty in emptiness is not stable yet.

Nagarjuna applies his analysis of meeting to the mental afflictions and the remaining sources of consciousness in the second verse:

> Desire, the desirous one, and the object of
>   desire do not meet either,
> Nor do any of the remaining afflictions,
> Nor any of the remaining sources of
>   consciousness:
> In these sets of three there is neither
>   meeting in pairs nor all together.

The contact between desire, the individual who experiences the desire, and the desired object, just like the meeting of object, faculty, and consciousness, is a mere appearance that occurs due to the coming together of causes and conditions—it is not the slightest bit real. The same can be said for anger, the angry individual, and the object of the anger, as well as for the other mental afflictions (pride, desire, and stupidity), those who experience them, and their objects. You should also apply this analysis to the remaining sources of consciousness: sound, the ear, and the ear sense consciousness, and the remaining four (nose, tongue, body, and mind) sets of three (object, sense faculty, and consciousness).

Concerning this, Mipham Rinpoche explains in his commentary,

"Sense objects, faculties, and consciousnesses meet neither in pairs nor all together, just like the son and daughter of a childless woman." This is a good example! It is an example coming from the perspective of object, faculty, and consciousness having no existent essence, an example from the perspective of their emptiness. From the perspective of their appearance, their meeting is an incidence of dependent arising, a mere coming together of causes and conditions, like in a dream. It is the union of appearance and emptiness. So there is no need to be afraid of emptiness meaning "nothingness," because it does not.

When we think that the meeting of object, faculty, and consciousness is real, suffering increases. In fact, you could say that most of the suffering in the world is the result of believing sense contact or the absence of sense contact to be truly existent. However, when we gain certainty that sense contact is a dependently arisen mere appearance, like in a dream, the quality of our meditation increases. Therefore, do not be attached to the meeting of object, faculty, and consciousness as being real. Know that the appearance of their meeting is illusory and dreamlike.

> For all ignorant beings without exception,
> Clinging to contact as being real increases
>   their suffering,
> So they are in need of instruction in the
>   practice
> Of self-liberation through recollection.

Our suffering increases in direct proportion to the extent that we cling to the meeting of object, faculty, and consciousness as being real. That is why the practice of self-liberation through recollection is so important.

In his song *The Eight Wonderful Forms of Happiness*, Milarepa sang of how he used this practice to cut the rope that binds perceived object and perceiving subject:

The meeting of appearances and the six
   kinds of consciousness—
This is the guide that turns adverse
   conditions into a path.
Is there anyone here who is able to keep to
   this path and follow it through?
The one for whom desire and craving self-
   liberate is happy.
The rope that ties perceiver and perceived
   when cut is emaho![21]

The connection between perceiver and perceived is not truly existent; it is a dependently arisen mere appearance. Therefore, we have
to cut the rope of clinging to duality as being real. The way to do
that is to reflect on the emptiness of the meeting of perceiver and
perceived with our precise knowledge of the genuine nature of
reality.

When we remember that the true nature of sense perceptions is
appearance-emptiness, our experience of them will be open, spacious, and relaxed. This is the method that turns experiences we
would otherwise consider to be adverse conditions into the path of
Dharma. We can begin to experience what we would otherwise consider to be painful and difficult as open, spacious, and relaxed, just
as we would experience the appearance of difficulty when we were
dreaming and we recognized that it was a dream. You need to train
in this again and again, first with minor experiences of suffering,
and then gradually you will be able to apply it even to experiences
of great suffering. Recognizing that both happiness and suffering
are mere conceptual imputations, and that therefore genuine reality
transcends them both, you will experience the inconceivable and
inexpressible equality of happiness and suffering, an experience that
is, as Milarepa sang, a most wonderful form of happiness.

21. *Emaho* is a Tibetan word that expresses surprise or amazement.

15

An Examination of Things and the Absence of Things

In the *Sutra Requested by the Bodhisattva "Shining Intelligence,"* the Buddha taught:

Forms are neither extinct nor permanent.

❖ ❖ ❖ ❖ ❖

PERMANENCE AND EXTINCTION, existence and nonexistence—these are just conceptual fabrications that cannot describe the genuine nature of reality. Therefore, the Buddha taught that forms' true nature transcends both permanence and extinction.

Nagarjuna composed this chapter in answer to those who claimed, "Things have an inherent nature because when their causes and conditions come together, they come into existence. When there is an absence of things, it is because causes and conditions have not come together to produce anything, as is the case with flowers in the sky." In this way, these people believed that the existence of things and the nonexistence or absence of things was real. In order to help them overcome this mistaken belief, Nagarjuna analyzes the existence of things and the absence of things and demonstrates that neither one has any inherent nature.

It is important to distinguish between the way things appear to the sense consciousnesses and the way they appear to the conceptual aspect of the mental consciousness. When sense consciousnesses perceive forms, sounds, smells, tastes, and tactile sensations, they do not think that there is something there, nor do they think that there is nothing there. They just perceive their objects nonconceptually. Then the mental consciousness comes along and thinks, for example, "I see something" or "I do not see that thing." It is thoughts, therefore, that conceive of there being something or nothing, not the sense consciousnesses. "Something" and "nothing" are therefore purely conceptual imputations. They are merely the fabrications of conceptual mind.

At the same time that thoughts are thinking, "There is something" or "There is nothing," the true nature of reality is beyond something and nothing. Something and nothing are only dependently existent. For example, if the entity of this earth really existed, it would have to exist independent of our idea of nothing, independent of our idea of space. It would have to exist objectively as a thing, independent of our thought of nothing. Similarly, space is the mere absence of things, and if it truly existed it would have to exist independent of our thought of the existence of things.

In reality, however, "something" and "nothing" must depend upon each other for their existence. You can only have a thought of something being there if you have a notion of what it means for nothing to be there, and vice versa. You can only have a thought of space, the absence of things, if you have some idea of what is missing, the thing that is absent. Therefore, whatever it may be, it cannot be said to be inherently existent or nonexistent—existence and nonexistence are just dependently existent concepts that our thoughts superimpose onto genuine reality, whose nature transcends all such fabrications.

In the seventh verse of this chapter, Nagarjuna states:

> In his *Pith Instructions to Katyayana,*
> The one who knows all things and all
>   absences of things,
> The Transcendent Conqueror,
> Refuted both existence and nonexistence.

The commentary quotes from this sutra called *The Pith Instructions to Katyayana* as follows:

> Katyayana, most people in the world fixate intensely on things as being existent, and others on the thought that things are nonexistent. As a result of their clinging, they are not free from birth, aging, sickness, or death; from agony, crying, suffering, mental anguish, or agitation. Especially, they are not free in any way from the torments of death.

> Teaching in this way, the Buddha refuted both extremes of existence and nonexistence.

The reason it is important for us to understand that the true nature of reality transcends both existence and nonexistence is that all of the suffering in the world comes from either the thought that there is something or the thought that there is nothing. For example, people who are wealthy have the suffering that goes along with having a lot of things, the suffering related to existence, while people who are poor have the suffering that comes from not having enough, the suffering related to nonexistence. That rich and poor both suffer, however, shows that neither type of suffering truly exists. If suffering truly came from having material things, then the rich would suffer but the poor would not; and if suffering truly came from not having material things, then the poor would suffer but the rich would not. Since both rich and poor suffer, however, this shows that their suffering has no real cause or inherent existence, that it is just the confused projection of conceptual mind.

In this way, we have to examine with our intelligence all the limitless kinds of suffering that can come from existence and nonexistence. We have to examine the actual reasons they occur and what their true nature really is.

This particular quote from *The Pith Instructions to Katyayana* is also important because it comes from the Vinaya teachings of the Shravakayana, and therefore all Buddhist schools must accept its validity.[22] No one can claim that it is not the authentic words of the Buddha. These days, the followers of the Shravakayana assert that the Mahayana sutras are not really the words of the Buddha, but rather that they are Nagarjuna's extensive commentaries on this passage that the Buddha spoke to Katyayana. They do not believe that the *Prajñāpāramitā Sutras* are the teachings of the Buddha himself. They say that those teachings are in fact Nagarjuna's extensive explanations of what the Buddha actually said in this teaching to Katyayana.

In verse ten, Nagarjuna instructs us how to train our minds in the Middle Way that is free from all extremes. This means that we have to realize with precise knowledge what *Middle Way* actually means. One can follow the Middle Way path by refuting all extremes, but one needs to be free from the concept of abiding in the middle in between the extremes as well. The verse reads:

> "Existence" is the view of permanence,
> "Nonexistence" is the view of extinction,
> Therefore, the wise do not abide
> Either in existence or in nonexistence.

22. The Vinaya is the set of teachings the Buddha gave on the subject of prescribed and proscribed conduct for those who hold vows of the various *yanas* (vehicles) of Buddhism.

The views of permanence and extinction have both coarse and subtle levels. The coarse view of extinction is to deny the existence of past and future lives and of karmic cause and result. The coarse view of permanence is to believe that this life is truly existent. The subtle view of extinction is to have any concept at all of nonexistence, while the subtle view of permanence is to have any notion at all of existence.

There are those who, when they think that things exist, do not know how to understand existence in terms of dependently arisen mere appearances. They think that existence means that there is something truly there. That is the extreme of permanence. Then there are others who believe that emptiness means total nonexistence, complete nothingness. That is the view of extinction, the other extreme. Understanding, however, that appearances are appearance-emptiness eliminates the extremes of both existence and nonexistence, in the following way: That appearances lack inherent nature eliminates the extreme of existence. With a water-moon, for example, not a single particle of the moon exists there in the water, so it cannot be called existent. At the same time, that appearances do appear due to the coming together of causes and conditions is undeniable, and this eliminates the extreme of nonexistence. For example, no one could deny the vivid appearance of the moon there in the water. Therefore, in order to follow the Middle Way that falls into neither the extreme of existence nor that of nonexistence, we must understand that all phenomena are the union of appearance and emptiness, like dreams, illusions, and water-moons. Along these lines, Karmapa Rangjung Dorje taught:

> The way that the wise ones assert things
>   to be
> Is that all phenomena are neither true nor
>   false,
> They are like water-moons.

16

An Examination of Bondage and Liberation

In the sutras, the Buddha taught:

> Forms do not arise, and therefore they are neither bound nor liberated.

❁ ❁ ❁ ❁ ❁

THE BUDDHA MADE SIMILAR STATEMENTS about sounds, smells, taste, bodily sensations, and so forth; and thus connecting this teaching with many other phenomena, he taught of the transcendence of bondage and liberation in a vast way.

That bondage and liberation appear to be real, that we think they are real, and that we seem to have further experiences that confirm our belief that they are real is still not enough to prove they are real, because all of this also happens in dreams. You may dream of being bound in iron chains and then being let out of them, or of being thrown into prison and then being set free. Your dream body was never born in the first place, however, and therefore there is nothing really there to be bound or liberated. Thus, dream bondage and liberation are mere appearances, not real in the slightest. The bondage and liberation that appear during the day are the same.

In Tibet, some Dharma practitioners were imprisoned for twenty years, but they say that it was a very good experience—that it helped their practice a lot. They were probably meditating on the transcendence of bondage and liberation!

In this chapter, Nagarjuna will prove the validity of this teaching with logical reasoning. The reason he composed this chapter was that there were people who thought, "Things do in fact have an inherent nature because we can perceive them to be bound in samsara or liberated in nirvana." They used the existence of bondage and liberation as their proof of the existence of things. Thus, in order to help them give up their mistaken belief in true existence, Nagarjuna had to demonstrate to them why bondage and liberation do not exist in the genuine nature of reality.

Mipham Rinpoche's commentary identifies two main sections in this chapter: first, a refutation of samsara and nirvana, and second, a refutation of bondage and liberation themselves. From the first section, the first verse of the entire chapter reads:

> If one asks, "Do the aggregates wander?"
> No, they do not, because permanent
>   aggregates could not wander,
> And impermanent aggregates could not
>   wander either.
> The same holds true for sentient beings.

This verse takes up the analysis in the following way: If samsara truly exists, there must be someone or something wandering around in it. If there is no one wandering in samsara, samsara cannot be real.

We can identify two possibilities for what the wanderer is: Either it is the set of five aggregates that constitutes the sentient being, or it is the sentient being who possesses these aggregates. Whichever of these two is wandering in samsara, it must be either permanent or impermanent if it truly exists. There is no other possibility.

First, let us examine the aggregates. It cannot be that permanent aggregates wander in samsara, because permanent aggregates would never change states or phases. They could not go from one life to another, even from one place to another, because they would be unchanging. Impermanent aggregates cannot wander in samsara either, because something that is impermanent ceases as soon as it arises—that is the definition of impermanence. If it remained the same for any period of time, it would be permanent, not impermanent. Something that is impermanent, therefore, has no time to go anywhere, because as soon as it arises, it disappears. Therefore, impermanent aggregates would have no time to wander around in samsara, because they would cease immediately after arising. Thus, neither permanent nor impermanent aggregates can wander in samsara, and since there is no other alternative for how the aggregates could be, it is logically impossible that the aggregates wander in samsara.

The same is true for sentient beings. There could not be permanent sentient beings that wander in samsara because such beings would never change in any way; impermanent sentient beings could not wander in samsara either, because the first instant they would exist and the second instant they would be gone. They could not go from one place to another, let alone one life to another, because they would not have time to do so. Thus, sentient beings cannot logically be the wanderers in samsara either.

Since it is logically impossible for either permanent or imperma-nent aggregates or sentient beings to wander in samsara, and since there is no other possibility for how they could be, the only conclu-

sion to draw is that no wanderer in samsara actually exists. Since no
wanderer in samsara actually exists, samsara does not truly exist
either. Samsara is not real; it is just a dependently arisen mere appearance.

The third verse presents another line of reasoning. It reads:

> If the individual really wandered from one
>   existence to the next,
> Then in between existences, there would be
>   no existence!
> With no existence and no appropriated
>   aggregates,
> What individual could possibly be
>   wandering?

If this life, the next life, and the transition in between the two
truly existed, then there would be an individual sentient being who
would appropriate one set of aggregates in this life, then leave them
behind, then appropriate another set of aggregates at the start of
the next life. In between the two, however, there would just be the
individual, the appropriator, without any appropriated aggregates.
The sentient being would not have any aggregates at all at that point.
That would be illogical, however, because there would be nothing
to call a sentient being if there were no aggregates to compose that
sentient being—there would be no body and no mind. The sentient
being is defined as the one who appropriates the aggregates, so how
could that appropriator exist without any aggregates to appropriate?

Take, for example, the situation of being a human in this life and
a god in the next life. In between dying as a human being and giving
up that set of aggregates and then being born as a god with a new
set, there would be an empty gap. Then the question is, during that
empty gap, what is it that is going around in samsara? It would be
illogical to posit anything, because there would be nothing there.
The whole notion of samsara as an uninterrupted continuum of

lifetimes would be inapplicable if things actually transpired in that way.

Someone might say, "In between the two existences there is the sentient being in the bardo, the intermediate state." It is fine to posit that, but the question would then be, what is there in between the time when one abandons the human aggregates and one appropriates the bardo aggregates? Sentient beings in the bardo still have aggregates, just of a more subtle variety than our own. So positing the existence of the bardo changes the form of the question but does not make it go away.

Let us look at the example of being a pig in the past life and a human being in this one. First you are a pig and then you are a person. So if you go from being a pig to being a human being, the question is, are the human being's aggregates the same as the pig's aggregates, or not? If they are the same, then that pig would be a permanent pig. If the aggregates were different, however, then you would first have the pig's aggregates, then you would have nothing at all, and then you would have the human being's aggregates. The human being's aggregates would have no cause, because they would have just emerged from that nothingness of the gap in between the two lives. Therefore, neither the possibility of permanence nor that of impermanence is feasible, and therefore samsara's existence is not feasible either. This becomes clear once we analyze with logical reasoning in this way.

Samsara is the beginningless cycle of existence in which sentient beings wander in the six realms from one lifetime to the next. We can see from this analysis, however, that samsara is just a dependently arisen mere appearance, like a dream. There is nothing real to it or in it. Since samsara is just a dependently arisen appearance, it is naturally open, spacious, and relaxed. Therefore, we do not have to cleanse ourselves of samsara, only of our thoughts that samsara truly exists.

In his *Authentic Portrait of the Middle Way*, Jetsün Milarepa sang, "So even the name 'samsara' does not exist." Not only the basis to which the name *samsara* is given does not exist, but even the name itself does not exist. After all, the name *samsara* is comprised of three syllables. When you say the first syllable, *sam*, then *sara* does not exist. When you say *sa*, however, *sam* and *ra* do not exist, and when you say *ra*, *samsa* does not exist. If the name really existed, all its parts would have to exist at the same time!

In fact, both the basis to which the name *samsara* is imputed as well as the name itself are appearance and emptiness undifferentiable. Milarepa described this when he sang in *The Eight Kinds of Mastery*:

> Not separating appearance and emptiness
> This is mastery of the view.

Thus, we can see that Milarepa's intention and Nagarjuna's intention are the same.

When someone argued, "Samsara truly exists because there is nirvana, the transcendence of samsara's suffering," Nagarjuna responded by analyzing nirvana in the fourth verse:

> No matter how they might be,
> It would be untenable for the aggregates to
>   attain nirvana.
> No matter how they might be,
> It would be untenable for sentient beings to
>   attain nirvana.

Nirvana does not truly exist because when we analyze, we cannot find anything or anyone that can actually attain it. For example, the aggregates cannot attain nirvana, because permanent aggregates could not change states—they could not go from the state of samsara to that of nirvana—and impermanent aggregates would arise and then immediately cease, so they would not have time to attain nirvana. Similarly, permanent sentient beings could not logically

attain nirvana because they would be unchanging, and impermanent sentient beings could not attain nirvana because they would
not have time to do so.

Another reason nirvana is not truly existent is that samsara and
nirvana are dependently existent. There can only be samsara in dependence upon there being nirvana, and there can only be nirvana
in dependence upon there being samsara. Since these two things
exist only in mutual dependence, they do not inherently exist.

It is for these reasons that in *An Authentic Portrait of the Middle
Way*, the Jetsun sang:

> No meditator and no meditated,
> No paths and levels traveled and no signs,
> And no fruition bodies and no wisdoms,
> And therefore there is no nirvana there,
> Just designations using names and
>   statements.

This whole passage is a logical reasoning that progresses in stages.
First, Milarepa sang that there is no meditator. There is no meditator because there is no self. If there is no meditator, there cannot be
any object of meditation, and if there is no object of meditation,
there cannot be any path or any signs of progress on the path. If
there is no path, there cannot be any fruition at the end of the path
in the form of the fruition bodies and wisdoms.[23] If there are no
fruition bodies or wisdoms, there is no such thing as nirvana. All of
these terms then are just designations, mere names and imputations.

The *Heart of Wisdom Sutra* teaches that there is "no path, no
wisdom, no attainment, and no nonattainment either." The teaching that is neither attainment nor any absence of attainment is a
perspective that we have to apply to the other subjects mentioned

---

23. "Bodies" is a translation of the Sanskrit *kaya*; for a description of the three kayas, see
notes 28 and 29, page 145.

as well. For example, there is neither a path nor any absence of a path, there is no wisdom nor any absence of wisdom, and so forth. The ultimate nature of reality transcends all concepts of what it might be.

The people who believed in the true existence of things next asserted that samsara and nirvana exist because bondage and liberation exist, so Nagarjuna responded by analyzing bondage and liberation themselves in the fifth verse:

> The aggregates, characterized by birth and
> decay,
> Are not bound and do not become free.
> Similarly, sentient beings
> Are not bound and do not become free.

It is very easy to see that permanent aggregates or sentient beings could not be bound and later liberated, so it was not necessary for Nagarjuna to explicitly mention that in this verse. What he does examine is the belief that impermanent aggregates could first be bound and then liberated. That is a mistaken notion, because impermanent aggregates would have the qualities of arising and ceasing moment by moment, and therefore they would not have time to be bound and then liberated. They would not have time to have these two different states because as soon as they arose they would immediately cease. Similarly, permanent sentient beings could not be bound or liberated, and impermanent sentient beings could not be bound and liberated either.

Sometimes it seems that we are terribly bound by the mental afflictions of desire, anger, jealousy, and so forth. However, Nagarjuna analyzes this in the sixth verse and demonstrates that the mental afflictions do not bind anyone at all:

> Do the mental afflictions bind?
> They do not bind one already afflicted,

And they do not bind one who is not
    afflicted,
So when do they have the opportunity to
    bind anyone?

If we think that the mental afflictions truly bind us, then the question is, in whom does their activity of binding begin? It cannot begin in those who are already afflicted—sentient beings—because once they are bound by the afflictions, it makes no sense that this bondage would have to begin anew. Furthermore, it cannot begin in those who are not bound by afflictions, like the buddhas, because the afflictions have no power to bind such realized beings. Thus, the afflictions cannot begin to bind anyone in the first place, so how could anyone actually be bound by them? In genuine reality, therefore, the mental afflictions do not bind anyone. The trouble they seem to cause is a mere appearance without the slightest reality to it, and since the afflictions do not bind anyone in the first place, there is actually no liberation from them either. Thus, genuine reality transcends the notions of bondage and liberation. Within it, nothing is ever bound and nothing ever set free.

Since it is the case that bondage and liberation are not real, then it is also the case that samsara and nirvana do not truly exist either. This is what Nagarjuna teaches in the tenth and final verse:

There is no nirvana to be produced
And no samsara to be cleared away.
In essential reality, what samsara is there?
What is there that can be called nirvana?

Since samsara and nirvana do not truly exist, there is no nirvana to be produced or attained and no samsara to be eliminated.

That there is no samsara to clear away and no nirvana to be produced is the result of phenomena lacking inherent existence. If things truly existed, there would in fact be a samsara to get rid of and a nirvana to attain. If things truly existed, it would be like that, but since they are in fact empty of their own essence, there is no samsara that we need to get rid of and no nirvana that we need to attain.

In a dream there can be appearances that we like, which we call "good," and other appearances that we do not like, which we call "bad." If things in a dream actually existed, the good appearances that we like and the bad appearances that we do not like would also truly exist. Since nothing in a dream has any true nature, however, then actually there is no good or bad. For this reason, bondage and liberation, samsara and nirvana, are taught to be equality.

Since the true nature of reality is the equality of being bound and being set free, it is called "originally free" or "primordially free," and the great siddhas have sung many songs of what the experience of realizing this original, primordial freedom is like. In fact, if you think, "Well, all of this intellectual analysis is just philosophy, just some type of intellectual exercise," that is incorrect, because the lord of yogis Milarepa sang about the exact same thing in *An Authentic Portrait of the Middle Way*, a song he sang out of the wisdom arising from his meditation.

Furthermore, when in the teachings of Mahamudra and Dzogchen it is said that neither samsara nor nirvana actually exists, those explanations rely on precisely these reasonings to establish their validity. Without these reasonings, we could never prove those teachings to be correct.

17

An Examination of Karmic Actions and Results

In the sutras, the Buddha taught:

> For those belonging to the family of the noble ones, karmic actions do not exist and results of karmic actions do not exist, either.

❖ ❖ ❖ ❖ ❖

THE NOBLE BUDDHAS AND BODHISATTVAS realize the emptiness of all phenomena, and therefore they realize that karmic actions and their results do not truly exist. As a result of their realization, they pass beyond the karmic actions and results that cause ordinary sentient beings to wander in samsara. In this chapter, Nagarjuna will use logical reasoning to prove the validity of the teaching that karmic actions and their results are not truly existent.

Nagarjuna composed this chapter in order to counter the argument that samsara exists because the karmic actions and their results
that compose samsara exist. For if people believe this, then until one
proves to them that there really are no such things as karmic actions
and results, they will not be able to gain certainty in the fact that
samsara itself has no inherent reality. It is true that if karmic actions
and their results really did exist, then samsara would as well, but if
karmic actions and their results do not genuinely exist, then samsara
must necessarily not truly exist either.

We can formulate the following logical reasoning: Karmic actions
and results are mere appearances devoid of true existence, because
no self, no actor, exists to perform them. This is a valid way to put
things because if the self of the individual does not exist, there cannot be any action, and therefore there cannot be any result of any
action either.

We can also examine the relationship between the actors and the
actions themselves by asking, "Which one comes first?" It could not
be that the actor exists first, because then there would be an actor
who was not performing any action. It also would be impossible for
there to be any action before the actor who performed it, because if
there were, there would be an action that existed even though no
one was performing it. Neither could actor and action exist simultaneously, because if they did, each with its own inherent nature, then
each would be independent of the other and thus they would have
no connection between them. If that were the case here, there would
be two separate entities, actor and action, existing simultaneously
with no connection between them, which would be illogical. So
actor and action cannot exist sequentially and they cannot exist simultaneously, and therefore they cannot genuinely exist.

If karmic actions and actors did truly exist, what would be the
quality of that existence? If the actor really existed, he would have
to have his own independent nature, which would mean that the
actor would always exist, whether there was an action or not. Similarly, if the action really existed, it would have to have its own inde-

pendent nature, meaning that it would not exist in dependence upon the actor at all—it would exist by itself. Obviously, though, that is not the case, because we can say that there is an actor only if there is an action, and we can say that there is an action only if there is an actor. Since these two exist only in mutual dependence, they therefore have no independent nature; they are not real.

Someone might ask, "Isn't it nihilistic to think that karmic actions and their results do not exist?" In fact, this is not a nihilistic view because there exists no self to have any nihilistic view. There can be a nihilistic view only if there is someone to hold it, but since there is no one to have any view, then there can be no nihilism. Furthermore, since the thought of nihilism neither arises nor abides nor ceases, there can be no nihilism in genuine reality. Genuine reality transcends the conceptual fabrications of realism and nihilism. It transcends karmic actions and results, and the absence of karmic actions and results as well.

If karmic actions and their results do not exist in the abiding nature of reality, then what is the quality of their appearance? Nagarjuna describes this in the chapter's thirty-third verse:

> Mental afflictions, actions, and bodies,
> As well as actors and results,
> Are like cities of gandharvas,
> Like mirages, and like dreams.

This verse teaches us that karmic actions and their results do not genuinely exist; they are mere conventions, mere superficial appearances, like cities of gandharvas, mirages, and dreams. Thus, even though actors and actions do not genuinely exist, in apparent reality they do exist as dependently arisen mere appearances. So you do not need to worry or be afraid of reality being nothingness. Reality is appearance and emptiness undifferentiable, and this appearance-emptiness is open, spacious, and relaxed.

The *Heart of Wisdom Sutra* teaches:

> There is no ignorance nor any ending of ignorance, no
> aging and death nor any ending of aging and death.

The sutra here explicitly mentions the first and the last of the twelve
links of dependent arising; we must ourselves apply this to the ten
middle links as well.[24]

If ignorance inherently existed, its ending would also inherently
exist. Since ignorance does not inherently exist, however, there is no
ending of it either. If aging and death inherently existed, there
would be some end to them as well, but since they have no nature
of their own, there can be no true cessation of them either. So what
are they? They are like dreams, illusions, and water-moons. Confusion, liberation, stains, and the freedom from stains are all dependently arisen mere appearances whose true nature is equality.

When we dream of first being filthy and then getting clean, when
we do not know we are dreaming, both the filth and the cleanliness
seem to truly exist. When we know we are dreaming, the filth is
mere appearance and the cleanliness is mere appearance. In the true
nature of the dream, there is neither filth nor cleanliness. That is
easy to understand—please do not forget it.

In his *Authentic Portrait of the Middle Way,* Milarepa sang:

> All animate, inanimate—the three realms
> Unborn and nonexistent from the outset,
> No base to rest on, do not coemerge,
> There is no karmic act, no maturation,
> So even the name "samsara" does not exist.

We need to remember this again and again. If in our studies we
connect the teachings of the great scholar Nagarjuna with those of
the great yogi Milarepa, then our understanding will become very
profound.

---

24. For a brief description of the twelve links of dependent arising, see chapter 26, "An
Examination of the Twelve Links of Existence."

18

An Examination of
Self and Phenomena

In the sutras, the Buddha taught:

Form is empty of the self of the individual and the self of
phenomena.

❀ ❀ ❀ ❀ ❀

THE STATEMENT HERE is specifically made with regard to form,
but it actually applies to every one of the inconceivable number of
phenomena that there are. In this chapter, Nagarjuna proves its validity with logical reasoning.

All the Buddha's teachings on emptiness can be included in the
descriptions of the selflessness of individuals and the selflessness of
phenomena. These two types of selflessness or emptiness are the
focus of this eighteenth chapter, and therefore it is like the heart of
the entire text.

Nagarjuna composed this chapter in response to the people who asked, "If actions, mental afflictions, actors, and so forth are all false appearances, then what is the true nature of reality after all?" To answer this question, Nagarjuna explains the two types of selflessness that are the essence of genuine reality.

The first four verses and the first line of the fifth are an exceptionally clear explanation of the selflessness of the individual. The first verse reads:

> If the self were the aggregates,
> It would be something that arises and
>   ceases.
> If the self were something other than the
>   aggregates,
> It would not have the aggregates'
>   characteristics.

In chapter 10, "An Examination of Fire and Firewood," Nagarjuna analyzed the five possible relationships between the self and the aggregates; here, those five are condensed into the two that form their essence. The question is, if the self exists, is it the same as or different from the five aggregates that compose the individual's body and mind?

First, the self cannot be the same as the aggregates, because if it were, it would arise and cease just as the aggregates do. For example, just as the parts of the body arise and cease moment by moment, so the self would be born and die moment by moment. Just as feelings change every instant, so the self would only last one instant and then be replaced by another self. Furthermore, if the self were the aggregates, then just as the aggregates are many in number, so there would be that many selves. Each part of the body would be a different self; each thought would be a different self. Finally, if the self were the aggregates, it could no longer be said to possess the aggregates. You could no longer say, "my head," "my thoughts," or "my feelings," because those statements assume that the self and the aggregates are different things.

The self cannot be different from the aggregates either, however, because if it were, it would not have any of the aggregates' characteristics. It would not take birth, live, or die, because all the things that arise, abide, and cease are included in the five aggregates. The self would not be able to perform any function, because everything that performs a function is included in the five aggregates. Rather than being a thing, it would be inert nothingness, like empty space.

Thus, the self is not the same as the aggregates, it is not different from the aggregates, and there is no other possibility for how the self could exist in relation to the aggregates. Therefore, the self does not truly exist. It is as simple as that. The second verse reads:

> If there is no "me" in the first place,
> How could there be anything that belongs
>   to me?
> When "me" and "mine" are found to be
>   peace,
> Clinging to "me" and "mine" ceases.

This verse is fairly easy to understand. Once we determine that there is no self, it necessarily follows that there is nothing belonging to the self. This shows us that all of our possessiveness and attachment to things we consider to be our own is just as confused as the thought that we really exist in the first place.

By listening to and reflecting upon these reasonings, however, we can develop the precise knowledge that "me" and "mine" do not genuinely exist, that their nature is peace, beyond conceptual fabrications. This precise knowledge is enough to put a stop to our confused clinging to them as being real, and in fact, there is no other way to do so. You cannot stop clinging to the belief in "me" and "mine" until you are certain that they do not exist; mere unsubstantiated faith in the Buddha's teachings on selflessness is not enough.

The stronger your precise knowledge in selflessness becomes, however, the weaker your clinging to the true existence of the self becomes, and the easier it is to use your knowledge of selflessness as a remedy for the mistaken belief in self whenever you notice it arising. When you apply this remedy, clinging to the belief in self dissolves in the open, spacious, and relaxed certainty that the self is a mere appearance, the union of appearance-emptiness. This is something you have to train in again and again.

Some people might argue, "There are yogis and yoginis who realize selflessness, and this proves that the self really does exist after all, or else who would be the ones who possessed this realization?" Nagarjuna answers this claim in the third verse:

> The ones who do not cling to "me" or
>   "mine"
> Do not exist either.
> Those who do not cling to "me" or "mine"
>   see accurately,
> So they do not see a self.

We can apply the analysis from the first verse to the yogis and yoginis who realize selflessness, and see that since they are neither the same as nor different from the aggregates, they do not truly exist either. Therefore, these realized beings are also dependently arisen mere appearances, conceptual designations that lack inherent nature. They are appearance-emptiness: That they appear does not cause them to be truly existent, and that they do not truly exist does not prevent them from appearing, just as is the case with appearances in dreams.

The last two lines teach how it is that yogis' and yoginis' realization of selflessness prevents them from clinging to themselves as being truly existent. Their realization also prevents them from feeling proud as a result of having accomplished it—since they know that there is really no one there who realized anything, what reason would there be to be proud? Conversely, as long as someone is proud of or attached to their accomplishments or meditative experiences, they should know that they have not yet realized selflessness.

The fourth verse and the first line of the fifth verse describe how realization of the selflessness of the individual leads to liberation from samsara:

> When one stops thinking of the inner and
>   outer aggregates as being "me" or
>   "mine"
> All wrong views disappear,
> And once they have disappeared, birth in
>   the cycle of existence stops.
>
> When karmic actions and mental afflictions
>   cease, that is liberation.

The inner aggregates constitute one's own body and mind, and the outer aggregates are everything on the outside that one does not conceive of as being part of oneself. Our mistaken concepts of these inner and outer aggregates as being "me" and "mine" are the root of samsaric suffering. When we believe in the true existence of "me" and "mine," that leads to thoughts of "I find this pleasant" and "I find this unpleasant," which are the roots of the mental afflictions of attachment and aversion, respectively. These mental afflictions motivate us to pursue what we find pleasing and shun what we find displeasing—in short, to perform the defiled karmic actions that result in the uninterrupted suffering of samsara.

When we realize the selflessness of the individual, however, this whole process stops. The wrong views that have their root in the belief in self cease, then the mental afflictions cease, then karmic actions cease, and as a result of that, birth in samsara's cycle of existence ceases. This cessation of compulsive birth in samsara is the liberation that is described as nirvana in the Shravakayana and

Pratyekabuddhayana. Once practitioners who follow those paths perfectly realize the selflessness of the individual, they attain the level of an arhat in "nirvana with remainder," because as long as they are still alive, they have the remainder of their defiled aggregates. When they pass from that final life, they attain the state of an arhat in "nirvana without remainder," leaving all their aggregates behind and entering the expanse of peace.

Bodhisattvas who realize the selflessness of the individual gain the same liberation from samsaric rebirth as the arhats do, but for them the outcome is different: They continue to take rebirth again and again in samsara, out of their love and compassion for sentient beings and their desire to lead them out of samsara as well. They are not satisfied simply to gain liberation for themselves—they want everyone to do so! As the bodhisattva Ngulchu Thogme writes in *The Thirty-seven Practices of a Bodhisattva*:

> From beginningless time, my mothers have
>   cherished me;
> What is the point of my happiness if they
>   are suffering?
> Therefore, in order to liberate limitless
>   sentient beings,
> To give rise to bodhichitta is the practice of
>   a bodhisattva.

Therefore, the bodhisattvas are delighted to take birth again and again in samsara. They do not suffer as a result of doing so, however, because they have realized the selflessness of the individual in the manner described above. How could they suffer when they know that no self exists to suffer? Realizing this, for them samsara is a delightful experience, and their work for the benefit of sentient beings is uninterrupted by thoughts of depression, discouragement, fear, or selfishness. This is why realizing the selflessness of the individual is so important.

To be able to benefit beings to the utmost, however, one must attain the state of omniscience, the state of buddhahood. In order to do that, one must perfect one's realization of the selflessness of phenomena, which is the next subject of the chapter.

There are several synonyms for that which is to be realized: "emptiness," "actual reality," "the expanse of genuine reality" (*dharmadhatu*), "essential reality" (*dharmata*), and "the precise nature of reality." Here, the last of these terms is used, and its characteristics are described in verse nine:

Unknowable by analogy; peace;
Not of the fabric of fabrications;
Nonconceptual; free of distinctions—
These are the characteristics of the precise
    nature.

These are the five parts of the definition of the precise nature of reality. It is called by this name to highlight that it is precisely that and nothing else. It is only genuine reality and nothing else.

First, the precise nature is "unknowable by analogy." The precise nature of reality transcends all conceptual fabrications, and therefore no example, sign, or expression can describe what it is. In fact, the only way to lead disciples to realize it is to describe what it is not. Thus, the Buddha taught that the precise nature neither arises nor ceases, is neither one nor many, does not come or go, and is neither existent nor nonexistent. These explanations cannot describe the precise nature directly, but they can help us to dissolve our conceptual fabrications of what it is, and this will lead to our direct experience of it. Experiencing it directly with the precise knowledge arising from meditation is the only way to realize it—it is impossible for someone else to demonstrate or show it to us.

Therefore, if it is something that concepts, terms, and examples can describe or identify, and we can thereby know it without the precise knowledge arising from meditation, it is not the precise nature of reality.

Second, it is "peace in its true nature." The precise nature is the peace that is naturally free from the four extremes of existence, nonexistence, both existence and nonexistence, and neither existence nor nonexistence. Therefore, if something can be said to fall into one of these four extremes, it is not the precise nature of reality.

Third, it is "not fabricated by fabrications." If speech can fabricate an expression of it as being "this" or "that," then it is not the precise nature. For if within it not even the slightest movement of conceptual mind stirs, what need to mention its transcendence of the contrivances of speech?

Fourth, it is "nonconceptual." It is not the object of conceptual mind, but rather of nonconceptual primordial wisdom. This is also taught by the bodhisattva Shantideva in his *Guide to the Bodhisattva's Conduct,* where he explains:

Genuine reality cannot be experienced by the intellect.

This is the case because genuine reality itself cannot be described by any conceptual fabrication, like existent, nonexistent, and so forth. Since no such label can apply to it, and since thoughts can only relate to things in terms of names and labels, then genuine reality cannot be known by the intellect, cannot be fathomed by conceptual mind. Therefore, if the intellect is conceiving of something, then whatever it is, it is not reality's precise nature.

Fifth and finally, the precise nature is "free of distinctions." There are not different things within it, because it is the equality of all opposites. Good and bad, enemy and friend, poor and rich, male and female, clean and dirty, suffering and happiness, and so forth— the precise nature is the equality of all these distinctions because it transcends them all. Therefore, if something falls into the category of one of these distinctions, it is not the precise nature of reality.

To summarize the teachings in this chapter, everything in samsara and nirvana is empty of the self of the individual and empty of the self of phenomena. It is all empty of inherent existence, and therefore the nature of genuine reality cannot be described. It is not an object of expression; it is beyond the conceptual fabrications of arising, abiding, and ceasing. This explanation is in harmony with those of the Mahamudra and Dzogchen traditions, in which there are many teachings on how it is that genuine reality is inexpressible and inconceivable. The reasonings that those teachings rely upon to prove their validity are none other than the ones in Nagarjuna's great text.

19

An Examination
of Time

In the *Sutras of the Mother*, the Buddha taught:

The past is imperceptible, the future is imperceptible, and the present is imperceptible. . . . The three times are equality.

❊ ❊ ❊ ❊ ❊

THE PAST AND THE FUTURE are not perceived by the eye of wisdom. We conceive of them, but they are nowhere to be found. Similarly, the present does not abide for even an instant, so it is not perceptible either.

Nagarjuna composed this chapter as a response to people who claimed that things exist because the three times exist. The designations of past, present, and future, they argued, are possible only because of the existence of composite things: In dependence upon there being things that have ceased, we designate the past; in dependence upon there being things that exist now, we designate the present; and in dependence upon there being things that have yet to arise, we designate the future. Since these three times exist, and they definitely do because the Buddha spoke of them, then the things that are their causes must also exist. This was their argument.

In fact, the three times have no perceptible existence; they are just conceptual imputations. This is something that one can understand quite easily by looking at the first verse of the chapter:

> If the present and the future depended on
>   the past,
> The present and the future would exist in
>   the past.

We can also change this verse to cover the other possible permutations:

> If the past and the future depended on the
>   present,
> The past and the future would exist in the
>   present.

> If the past and the present depended on the
>   future,
> The past and the present would exist in the
>   future.

If the three times exist, they must either exist in dependence upon each other or independent of each other. If the first were the case, then, for example, if the present and the future existed in dependence upon the past, then the absurd consequence would be that the present and the future would have to exist in the past. This is the case because in order for one thing to depend upon another, the two have to meet. If only one exists at a time, it has nothing to depend upon, and there would be nothing there to depend upon it.

If they existed independent of each other, the absurd consequence of that would be that the present would exist independent
of any notion of the past or the future, and the past and the future
would exist independent of any notion of the present. If that were
the case, then we would have to conclude that the present is not
really the present after all, because it is something that does not
depend upon the past and the future. The fact is that if we have a
notion of the present, the only way we can do so is if we have some
idea of past and future. Even if something is called the present, if
it does not depend on past and future, it cannot actually be the
present.

If the present exists in dependence upon the past and the future,
however, then the present would exist both in the past and in the
future, because it would have to coexist with the thing that it depends upon for its existence. So the present would have to exist in
the past in order to depend on the past—it would have to exist in
the future in order to depend on the future.

Analyzing in this way makes it clear that the three times do not
truly exist, that time is just a creation of our thoughts. When we are
enjoying ourselves, for example, time seems to pass very quickly.
When we are suffering, it seems to pass excruciatingly slowly. Finally, when we are in deep sleep, we have no concept of time at
all—time simply does not exist for us in that state. So how does
time really pass after all? Does it pass quickly, slowly, or not at all?
There is no way to answer that question objectively.

These days, it is also easy to gain direct experience of the unreality
of time—just call a friend of yours in another country and ask what
time it is! Your friend might say, "It is twelve noon," and you might
say, "No, it is ten o'clock at night." Who would win that debate?
That people in different places in the world can have different ideas
of what time it is shows that time is just a mere appearance arisen
due to the coming together of causes and conditions. It is merely an
imputation of thoughts.

If time really existed, we would be able to perceive it independent of forms, sounds, smells, tastes, and tactile sensations. It would exist on its own, and we would be able to perceive it. The fact is, however, that time can exist only in dependence upon there being something to which we can relate the notion of time. For example, if nothing had ceased, we could have no notion of the past; if there were nothing here, we could have no notion of the present; and if we did not anticipate anything happening, we could have no notion of the future. Since time can exist only in dependence upon these things, it cannot truly exist.

In Chandrakirti's text *Entering the Middle Way*, he explains, "The present does not abide; the past and the future do not exist." Out of the sixteen emptinesses, the emptiness of time is "the emptiness of the imperceptible." When we look for time directly, this is what we find—time is imperceptible. Try it now—look at your watch. When you look at your watch to see what time it is, do you see time? No, you just see some small sticks moving around! When you look for it, you can never see time, because time is imperceptible. Time is emptiness.

Realizing the emptiness of time is important to our practice for several reasons. First of all, in the Mahamudra tradition, attachment to the three times as being real is called a wrong view. If we do not reverse our thought that time is real, we will not be able to realize equality.

Furthermore, realizing the true nature of time prevents us from getting attached to the length of time that we practice as being real. Some people think that they need to meditate for long periods of time or else it is not really Dharma practice. Others feel proud because they think they have been practicing Dharma for a certain number of years and are advanced practitioners as a result. Others get disappointed because they think they have been practicing for a long time and do not see any improvement in their situation—they might get so disappointed that they abandon Dharma practice altogether. Still others are in a big hurry and think that they have to achieve enlightenment as soon as possible. Realizing that time is not truly existent and that long and short periods of time are equality frees us from all of these types of attachment and the mental agitation that they cause. This freedom from attachment is open, spacious, and relaxed.

Realizing the true nature of time is particularly important for bodhisattvas, who vow to liberate every single one of the infinite number of sentient beings from samsara, no matter how many aeons that might take. Since they are free from attachment to long or short periods of time as being real, however, they can make that commitment quite eagerly and happily. As the Buddha taught, "an aeon and an instant are equality," and knowing this, bodhisattvas are able to remain in samsara and continuously perform deeds that benefit sentient beings without ever getting tired or discouraged.

All these reasons show why it is so important to realize that time is of the nature of appearance-emptiness, and the way we can do so is to use the logical reasonings presented in this chapter. Once we gain certainty in the emptiness of time, remembering it again and again will cause our certainty to become more and more stable, and then eventually we will realize the true nature of time directly. That is how the process works.

20

An Examination of Collections

In the sutras, the Buddha taught:

All the many things in the universe
Are appearances of collections.
Therefore, things themselves do not exist
And collections of things do not exist either.

❀ ❀ ❀ ❀ ❀

A FOREST, A HEAD OF HAIR, a woven tent, a garland of beads, and an army—these are all examples of collections. Collections are not real, because although the parts that compose the collection are there, the entity of the collection itself does not exist. When we look at a forest, for example, there really is no "forest;" there are just the trees. Whatever thing it might be in samsara or nirvana, it is also just a collection of smaller things that are its parts, and the thing itself that is said to possess the collection of parts, like the forest, does not exist.

It is good to apply this analysis to the body. The body is a collection of parts and is called the possessor of its parts. When we look, however, we see only the parts; no entity of the "body," the possessor of the parts, can be found. For this reason, the body does not truly exist. We should examine the parts too—let us take the hand, for example. The hand is a collection of joints. Since, however, no possessor of the collection of joints exists, the hand does not have any inherent nature. The finger can be analyzed in the same way, as can its components, down to the most subtle particles of matter. They are all merely collections, and therefore they all lack inherent existence.

People also come together in groups all the time, but these groups are constantly prone to change and decay. This is because whatever group it is, the entity of the group itself has no inherent existence.

Nagarjuna composed this chapter in answer to those people who said to him, "Your refutations aside, time does in fact exist because it is one part of the collection of conditions that cause the arising of a result. For example, when a seed, the five elements, and time all come together, a sprout can arise. As the Buddha taught, 'When the collection of causes gathers and the time is right, the precise result will occur.' Therefore, since collections of causes exist, and this collection includes time, then time must also exist."

Thus, it was necessary for Nagarjuna to demonstrate with logical reasoning why collections do not truly exist. He could have just asked these people nicely, "Please do not believe in the true existence of collections," but that would not have been enough. On the other hand, it is the case in general that if one can logically prove something to someone else, if they are intelligent and open-minded, they will accept it.

Taking a look at the above argument, it is certainly the case that in order for a flower to arise, all of the causes and conditions of that flower have to come together in a collection. There have to be the

seed, soil, fertilizer, water, heat, oxygen, and space—all of these have
to come together for the flower to arise. However, apart from these
individual elements, nothing we could call "the collection" exists.
This is because, apart from the individual elements, nothing else is
visible. No entity of the collection can be seen. Therefore, the flower
that appears to be the result of this collection of causes and conditions does not truly exist either, because the collection itself does
not truly exist in the first place.

The nineteenth verse in the chapter examines causes and results
from a different perspective, showing that causes and results cannot
be the same thing nor can they be different things, and therefore
they cannot genuinely exist:

> If cause and result were one,
> Then producer and produced would be the
>   same thing.
> If cause and result were different,
> Then causes and noncauses would be
>   equivalent.

Here we have to consider causes and results in a way that we are
not used to doing. We will not consider the continuum of the cause
to be just one thing and the continuum of the result to be one thing,
because that would be mere conceptual imputation. For example, it
is just a concept that takes the whole continuum of individual moments of a seed and turns it into one undifferentiated seed, or the
whole continuum of distinct moments of a sprout and turns it into
just one sprout. Here we will analyze in a more subtle way than our
thoughts ordinarily do, by looking at the very last instant of the seed
and the very first instant of the sprout that arises from it.

If the last moment of the seed and the first moment of the sprout
were the same thing, then cause and result would be one thing. The
cause would be the result; the result would be the cause. "Producer
and produced would be the same thing," as Nagarjuna describes.

That would not make sense, however, because from our own direct experience we know that cause and result are not the same thing. When the sprout exists, for example, the seed is nowhere to be found. If cause and result were the same thing, the seed should be visible at the time of the sprout, and, for that matter, the sprout should be visible at the time of the seed. Since it is not like that, we can conclude that seed and sprout, cause and result, are not one undifferentiated entity.

On the other hand, even though the last moment of the seed and the first moment of the sprout appear to be different things, if they were truly different from each other, they would be two independent entities that would have no connection between them. The result of that would be that since everything that was not a cause of the sprout would have no connection with the sprout, and since the seed that is the cause of the sprout would have no connection with the sprout either, then causes and noncauses would be equivalent in their lack of connection to the result, and therefore both should be equally able to produce the sprout. If a cause that is completely different from and has no connection to its result can nevertheless produce that result, what should stop a noncause that is completely different from and has no connection to the result from producing it as well?

The point is that when causes are posited as being different from their results, the distinction between what is a cause and what is not a cause of any specific result disappears. Generally in the world, we think that causes and their results have some connection or relation between them, and that is why one thing can produce a certain result but another thing cannot. Take that connection away, however, and the reason one thing can produce a certain result and others cannot disappears. Thus, when causes and results are different from each other, all things become equally able to give rise to everything else. Since this is not the case, as we can see in our own experience, for cause and result to be different from each other would also be impossible.

Related to the view that cause and result are the same is the idea that even though the cause itself does not exist at the time of the result, the cause somehow transfers its essence to the result, and therefore there is a continuity of this essential nature from the cause to the result that it produces. This would be like an actor in a play who just changes clothes from act to act, while remaining the same person throughout the whole performance—some essence, whatever that might be, would manifest at one stage as a seed and another stage as a sprout, while it itself would remain the same thing all the while, transferring itself from one stage to the next. This, however, is the view of permanence, and it is completely untenable, because if there were some permanent essence that continued to exist from one stage to the next, it would not arise from or be affected by causes and conditions. Whatever arises from causes and conditions is necessarily impermanent, ceasing immediately after it arises, as it is replaced by the result of a new set of causes and conditions. If that unchanging essence did not arise from causes and conditions, it could not perform the function of producing the result, for no causes and conditions would have given it the ability to do so. If it did not have the ability to produce the result, it would not have any relation with the cause, because its characteristics would be precisely the opposite of those of the cause, which is defined by its ability to produce a result.

On the other hand, and related to the view that cause and result are different things, is the idea that the cause ceases and then the result arises. This view, however, connotes the extreme of extinction—it posits that the cause vanishes and becomes nonexistent. If the seed first ceased and then the sprout arose, the sprout would not really have a cause, because first the seed would exist, then it would cease, then there would be nothing, and then the sprout would arise—but where would the sprout come from? It would come from out of nothingness, after its cause had ceased. So this view is not tenable either.

Finally, there is the view that the cause neither exists at the time of the result nor ceases before the result arises, but rather that the cessation of the cause and the arising of the result occur simultaneously. This is actually how it seems to happen in apparent reality: It seems that the seed ceases and the sprout arises precisely at the same moment. From the perspective of genuine reality, however, this view is also untenable, because arising and ceasing themselves are just conceptual imputations that do not accurately describe genuine reality. Positing simultaneous arising and ceasing does not help to get around the fundamental problem that cause and result cannot exist at the same time, nor can they exist sequentially, and therefore they cannot truly exist. For in the situation in which the cause's ceasing is simultaneous with the result's arising, when the cause is "ceasing" it still exists; but what about the result that is in the process of "arising"? Does the result exist when it is arising, or not?

If the result does exist when it is arising, and the arising of the result and the cessation of the cause occur simultaneously, then both cause and result would exist at the same time. This, however, is logically impossible, because then cause and result would be separate and independently existent entities that would have no connection with each other. Furthermore, if the result existed at the same time as its cause, the cause would have no opportunity to produce the result because the cause and result would come into existence simultaneously. If the result does not exist when it is arising, however, then what in fact would be arising? Arising without something there to arise makes no sense. Therefore, this view that posits the simultaneous cessation of the cause and arising of the result also falls apart under analysis.

Thus, it is not possible that the cause exists at the time of the result, nor that it does not exist at the time of the result. The Middle Way, therefore, does not assert either of these two views, and in this way it is free from the extremes of permanence and extinction, existence and nonexistence.

Then what of the appearance of the sprout arising from the seed, of results arising from the collections of causes and conditions?

These appearances are not real—they are mere instances of dependent arising. They are the same as what occurs when the night sky is free of clouds, a lake is clear and still, and, as a result, a water-moon vividly shines. As the siddha Gyalwa Gotsangpa sang in his vajra song of realization *The Eight Flashing Lances*:

> The murkiness of clinging clarified,
> Causes and conditions like reflections,
> Knowing what to do and not, that subtle
>   art—
> These three make dependent arising fully
>   free,
> Like a lance that flashes free in the open
>   sky.

When one is free of the murkiness of clinging to things as being real, causes and conditions shine like reflections in clear pools of water, as vivid manifestations of appearance-emptiness. Knowing them to be this way, one gains precise knowledge of what to do and what not to do. Thus, understanding the true nature of appearances does not impede good conduct; rather, it informs good conduct. Such knowledge makes conduct more subtle and beneficial. It is just like when you stand in front of a mirror and the reflection of your face appears within it. Knowing all the while that the reflection is not real, you can still use that reflection to remove stains from your face and make yourself look beautiful.

21

An Examination of Emergence and Decay

In the sutras, the Buddha taught:

O Bodhisattva of Shining Intelligence, forms do not die and they are not born.

❖ ❖ ❖ ❖ ❖

JOINING THIS WITH MANY OTHER SUBJECTS, the Buddha taught of the freedom from birth and death in a vast way.

Nagarjuna composed this chapter in answer to the proponents of the true existence of things who argued, "Your refutations of time aside, sprouts wither in the winter and emerge again in the spring, and in this way, time is the cause of emergence and decay. Therefore, if emergence and decay exist, time, which is their cause, must also exist." Thus, in order to prove to these people that time does not truly exist after all, Nagarjuna had to demonstrate logically that emergence and decay are not real.

One way to analyze emergence and decay is by asking, "If emergence and decay exist, are they the same thing or different things?" Nagarjuna gives the answer in verse ten:

> Emergence and decay
> Cannot logically be the same thing.
> Emergence and decay
> Cannot logically be different things.

Emergence and decay are not the same thing because they are opposites, like light and dark, heat and cold, and big and small. To say that something is emerging is the opposite of saying that it is decaying, just like saying that something is getting bigger is the opposite of saying that it is getting smaller. They cannot be different things either, because if they were, they would exist independent of each other. This they cannot do, because emergence can occur only in dependence upon decay, and decay can occur only in dependence upon emergence.[25] Furthermore, when considering the emergence and decay of a single entity, for example, a flower, since they both occur in relation to the same flower, how could they be different? How could they occur independent of each other? If they did, they would have to occur in completely different things.

This logical reasoning as well as the other ones in this chapter were still not enough to satisfy Nagarjuna's opponents, who argued further, "What is the point of all your subtle analysis? Everyone from uneducated shepherds on up sees emergence and decay happening with their own eyes! This direct experience is enough to prove that emergence and decay are real, no matter what your analysis may find." Nagarjuna replied to this claim in verse eleven:

---

25. For more on why emergence and decay exist only in dependence upon each other, see the similar analysis of arising, abiding, and ceasing in chapter 7, "An Examination of the Composite."

> When you think you see emergence and
>   decay,
> It is only bewilderment that sees emergence
>   and decay.

Just as in a dream, the apparently direct perception of emergence and decay is not enough to establish them as being truly existent. Just as in a dream when we do not know we are dreaming, it is only the veil of our bewilderment that causes us to think that the mere appearances of emergence and decay are real.

So shepherds may know quite a bit about the mode of appearance of their sheep, but that does not mean that they know the sheep's true nature. It is not really correct to say that shepherds are uneducated, though, because shepherds have to study a lot! They have to know all about their sheep: what the mother ewes are like, what the baby lambs are like, and what to do if some of the flock get sick. They also have to know how to protect their sheep from wolves and other dangers; in Western countries, shepherds have sheepdogs to help them do this job, but in Tibet, they had to do it themselves. So it is not really fair to call shepherds uneducated—good shepherds have to be very skillful! The most skillful shepherds know that their sheep are appearance-emptiness inseparable, and that their birth, aging, sickness, and death are as well. Those kinds of shepherds take the best care of their sheep, and they have a great time doing so!

22

An Examination of the Tathagata

In the sutras, the Buddha taught:

> The Tathagata is a phenomenon that never arises, and all other
> phenomena are similar to the Sugata.[26]

❖ ❖ ❖ ❖ ❖

JUST AS THE TATHAGATAS of the three times are ultimately unborn,
so all other phenomena are the same.

Nagarjuna composed this chapter in response to those who argued, "Samsara exists because the tathagatas, the buddhas, exist.
The tathagatas are the ones who gain liberation from samsara, and
since they exist, then the samsara that they transcend by attaining
enlightenment must also exist."

---

26. *Tathagata*, meaning "The Thus Gone One," and *Sugata*, meaning "The One Gone to
Bliss," are epithets for the Buddha.

To help these people overcome their mistaken belief in the true existence of samsara, Nagarjuna proves in this chapter that the Buddha does not truly exist, for if the Buddha does not truly exist, then samsara does not truly exist. Similarly, for samsara to be unreal while the Buddha was real would be illogical. To assert that all phenomena do not truly exist except for the Buddha who does truly exist would be illogical. For if sentient beings did not exist and the Buddha did, the Buddha would have no work to do because there would be no sentient beings to benefit!

The eleventh verse of the chapter reads:

> The Tathagata cannot be called "empty,"
>   nor "not empty," nor both, nor neither.
> Use these terms as mere conventional
>   designations.

At the stage when there is no analysis of the true nature of reality, the Buddha exists. At the stage of slight analysis, when precise knowledge examines the Buddha, it cannot find anything, and therefore it is explained that from the perspective of the eye of wisdom, the Buddha does not exist. At the stage of thorough analysis, one discovers that the actual nature of reality transcends both the existence and the nonexistence of the Buddha. No conceptual fabrications can apply. This is what the first line of this verse teaches. Nevertheless, as it says in the second line, "Use these terms as mere conventional designations," which means that even though none of these expressions of "empty," "not empty," "both empty and not empty," and "neither empty nor not empty" can describe genuine reality, still, sometimes it is good to explain that the Buddha exists, sometimes it is good to explain that the Buddha does not exist, and sometimes it is good to explain that the true nature of the Buddha transcends all conceptual fabrications.

To those who do not believe in the Buddha at all, who have no confidence that there is such a thing as enlightenment, it is good to explain that buddhahood exists as the ultimate result of the path of the cultivation of wisdom and compassion. We can explain that there is a path of wisdom and compassion, and when one reaches the culmination of that path, when one actualizes the ultimate perfection of these two qualities, then one is the Buddha. So the Buddha exists as the result of this path of wisdom and compassion, and it is good to explain things in this way to those people. There are many logical proofs of the existence of this path and its result.

To those who believe that the Buddha truly exists, it is good to explain that when one analyzes logically, no Buddha can actually be found. One cannot find any existence of the Buddha, and in fact Buddha Shakyamuni himself said that the Buddha does not truly exist. Explaining things in this way helps people to let go of their clinging to the Buddha as being real. In fact, the only way to stop thinking that things exist is to develop certainty that they do not exist. When meditating on emptiness, therefore, one must first meditate on the nonaffirming negation[27] of existence that leaves nothing remaining—emptiness that is like space.

This, however, is still a conceptual fabrication of emptiness, and as such it obscures our vision of the true nature of reality beyond conceptual fabrications. Therefore, to those who cling to the belief that the Buddha is empty or nonexistent, it is good to explain how, in the ultimate sense, reality transcends all conceptual fabrications. It is good to explain how the Buddha neither exists, nor does not exist, nor is some combination of the two, nor is something that is neither of them. This will help them to give up their clinging to the notion of the Buddha's emptiness and to realize the true nature of the Buddha, beyond all notions of what it might be.

When you dream and you know that you are dreaming, do you

27. A nonaffirming negation is a negation of existence that does not affirm the existence of anything in its place. For example, the statement "There is no spoon" merely negates the existence of a spoon without affirming the existence of anything else. This is opposed to an affirming negation, such as the statement "The lion is not dead." Negating death here implicitly affirms that the lion is alive.

think of yourself as existent? As nonexistent? As both? Or as neither? How do you think of yourself at that time? This type of analysis will help you to understand the meaning of this verse.

Thus, the first step is to see what perspective people are taking in terms of these four conceptual extremes. They might think that the Buddha exists or does not exist, or both exists and does not exist, or neither exists nor does not exist. Then, depending upon their conceptual perspective, the teacher explains to them from one of the three stages of analysis—either that the Buddha exists, or that the Buddha does not exist, or that the Buddha's nature transcends both existence and nonexistence. We have to see which perspective it is important to explain at that point, or else we will not be able to be of benefit. Therefore, we have to know: What are the reasons one can say that the Buddha exists? What are the reasons one can say that the Buddha does not exist? Finally, what are the reasons one can say that the Buddha transcends existence and nonexistence?

The twelfth verse refutes the extremes of permanence and impermanence and of finity and infinity:

> Permanent, impermanent, and so forth, the
>   four—
> Where are they in this peace?
> Finite, infinite, and so forth, the four—
> Where are they in this peace?

Peace here refers to the true nature of enlightenment, the true nature of the Tathagata. In this nature, the ultimate nature of reality, where is there any permanence or impermanence? Where is there some combination of the two or the absence of the two? Similarly, where is there finity or infinity? Where is there something that is both? Where is there something that is neither?

Depending on what is necessary at the time, it is both permissible and important to describe the Buddha as permanent, impermanent, or transcending both permanence and impermanence. These are the three main stages. For example, someone may think, "Well, the Buddha died, so the Buddha is not here now. The Buddha does not exist now because the Buddha is impermanent." If someone thinks like that, then the explanation to give is that the dharmakaya of natural purity is permanent and unchanging.[28] The dharmakaya of natural purity is nothing other than the Buddha, and therefore the Buddha is permanent. The Buddha is precisely the natural purity of reality's basic essence, which never ceases to exist.

On the other hand, if people cling to the notion that the Buddha is permanent, then they need the explanation from the perspective of the form kayas, which is that even the Buddha passes into nirvana.[29] Even the Buddha dies. So that is the way these two explanations are used, depending upon the way a person thinks. In fact, the true nature of reality transcends both the permanence and the impermanence of the Buddha. That is the actual nature of reality. It is the same with thinking about things being either finite or infinite—the same analysis applies.

The sixteenth verse of the chapter reads:

Whatever is the nature of the Tathagata,
That is the nature of wandering beings.
The Tathagata has no inherent nature;
Wandering beings have no inherent nature.

The nature of the tathagatas is beyond any concept of what it might be. It is completely free of any stain. It is originally pure.

---

28. The *dharmakaya* is one of the three kayas, or dimensions of enlightenment. The other two are the *sambhogakaya* and *nirmanakaya* (described in note 29). The dharmakaya refers to the Buddha's enlightened mind, and the dharmakaya of natural purity is the true nature of that enlightened mind, as well as the true nature of the mind of every sentient being. In its nature it transcends conceptual fabrication; it is the essence of genuine reality. When one realizes its nature perfectly, one attains the dharmakaya free of fleeting stains, awakening into the complete and perfect enlightenment of buddhahood.

29. There are two form kayas, the sambhogakaya and the nirmanakaya. The former appears to and teaches exclusively the noble bodhisattvas on the ten bodhisattva grounds; the latter appears to and teaches ordinary sentient beings and noble bodhisattvas alike.

That, precisely, is the nature of sentient beings—completely beyond concept, completely free of stains, pure from the very beginning. The true nature of the Tathagata and the true nature of sentient beings are exactly the same.

Samsara and nirvana are equality—in their true nature, they are the same. This is what is taught in Mahamudra and Dzogchen, and just as it is taught that samsara and nirvana are equality, so it is with buddhas and sentient beings—they are equality.

23

An Examination of Mistakes

In the *Prajñāpāramitā Sutras*, the Buddha taught:

Desire is perfectly pure, and therefore forms are perfectly pure.

❀ ❀ ❀ ❀ ❀

CONNECTING THIS WITH other mental afflictions and confused concepts:

Aversion is perfectly pure, and therefore forms are perfectly pure.

Pride is perfectly pure, and therefore forms are perfectly pure.

Stupidity is perfectly pure, and therefore forms are perfectly pure.

Jealousy is perfectly pure, and therefore forms are perfectly pure.

Wrong views are perfectly pure, and therefore forms are
   perfectly pure.
Doubts are perfectly pure, and therefore forms are perfectly
   pure.

Thus the Buddha taught about perfect purity in a vast way.

The reason Nagarjuna composed this chapter was that there were
those who said, "Samsara exists because the mistakes that produce
it exist. Mental afflictions cause sentient beings to accumulate
karma, and as a result they take birth again and again in samsara."
In order to help these people overcome their confused belief in the
reality of samsara, Nagarjuna had to present an analysis of the mistakes that produce samsara: mistaken concepts about reality; the
mental afflictions arising from these mistaken concepts; and the karmic actions motivated by these mental afflictions. Nagarjuna had to
demonstrate that none of these things truly exist.

   In general, people have a tendency to believe that being mistaken
and being unmistaken, being right and being wrong, are real. People
conceive of right and wrong as being opposites that truly exist. If
we are not able to reverse this tendency to think that right and
wrong are truly existent, it will be impossible for us to realize emptiness. This is why it is very important for us to analyze mistakes and
determine their true nature.

   It is also the case that sometimes people think, "I really do not
understand this stuff and all my views are wrong. I am constantly
thinking about things wrongly, I have all these bad thoughts, and I
have so many doubts. I am never going to attain enlightenment."
In this way, they get very discouraged. At other times people think,
"Look at that guy. He does everything wrong. His views are completely wrong. His conduct is completely wrong." This type of
thought is wrong in itself, though, for how could anyone know for
certain what is inside another person's mind? Therefore, in order to
reverse our tendency to get discouraged ourselves, as well as our

tendency to have wrong views concerning others, it is important for us to examine the true nature of mistakes.

To put this into verse:

> So that we are no longer discouraged by
>   our own bad thoughts, and
> So that we no longer incorrectly judge
>   others to have bad thoughts,
> Let us examine mistakes' true nature.

We can begin by examining the mental afflictions that arise as a result of mistaken thoughts and that cause us to take mistaken actions. The main mental afflictions are desire or attachment, aversion, and stupidity. Desire's referent object, what it focuses on, is something we consider pleasant. Aversion's referent object is something we find unpleasant, and stupidity's referent object is a mistake, a wrong view. Therefore, what we need to examine are these three objects: those we consider pleasant, those we consider unpleasant, and mistakes.

When we examine these objects, however, we cannot find anything really there at all. Whatever object we analyze, we find that it is merely imputed to exist in dependence upon its parts. Analyzing the parts themselves, we find that they too are imputed to exist in dependence upon their own parts. Down to the subtlest particles of matter imaginable, nothing has any type of existence other than as a mere dependent imputation. Therefore, since there really is no object out there, no reference point for any notions of pleasant or unpleasant, pleasant and unpleasant themselves cannot exist. This is what Nagarjuna teaches in the ninth verse:

> How could it be possible for
> Sentient beings who are like illusions
> Or objects that are like reflections
> To be either pleasant or unpleasant?

To put this in the form of a logical reasoning: Pleasant and unpleasant do not truly exist, because the bases for the respective notions of pleasant and unpleasant are individuals and objects that
themselves are appearance-emptiness, like illusions and reflections.
If there is no support or basis that can have these qualities of pleasant and unpleasant, then how can the qualities themselves really
exist? They cannot.

Another way to analyze is to look at the very notions of pleasant
and unpleasant themselves. Pleasant and unpleasant could truly
exist only if they did so independent of each other. However, pleasant cannot inherently exist before there is any notion of unpleasant,
because it would have no reference point. Pleasant has no reference
point in the absence of unpleasant. Similarly, unpleasant cannot
exist in the absence of pleasant, because it would have no reference
point. You cannot have a thought of something being unpleasant
without a thought of what pleasant means as well. Therefore, pleasant depends for its existence on unpleasant, but unpleasant itself
depends on pleasant to exist. Therefore, neither one truly exists, as
Nagarjuna teaches beginning with the tenth verse:

> We imagine something to be pleasant
> Based on our idea of what is unpleasant.
> But unpleasant too does not exist
>   independent of pleasant.
> Therefore, for pleasant to truly exist would
>   be impossible.

Pleasant does not truly exist because the concept of unpleasant that
it must depend upon for its existence in turn depends upon it—
pleasant—for its existence. The very thing pleasant exists in dependence upon must depend upon pleasant itself in order to exist.
Therefore, pleasant is not real.

The eleventh verse demonstrates the lack of inherent existence of
unpleasant:

> We imagine something to be unpleasant
> Based on our idea of what is pleasant.
> But pleasant too does not exist independent
>   of unpleasant.
> Therefore, for unpleasant to truly exist
>   would be impossible.

Unpleasant has no nature of its own because the concept of pleasant that it must depend upon for its existence in turn depends upon it in order to exist. So the very thing that unpleasant depends on in fact depends upon it. Therefore, unpleasant is not real either.

We can examine clean and unclean in the same way. Clean exists only in dependence upon unclean. Unclean exists only in dependence on clean. So they exist only in dependence upon each other, and therefore they cannot truly exist. If one thing depends upon something else, but that other thing must depend upon it, then neither one can really exist. Long and short, hot and cold, good and bad, happiness and unhappiness are all exactly the same. They are dependently existent and therefore they are not truly existent.[30]

In the twelfth verse, Nagarjuna describes how it is that since neither pleasant nor unpleasant exists, neither do the afflictive emotions of desire and aversion that appear to arise from contact with pleasant and unpleasant things:

> Since pleasant does not exist, how could
>   desire exist?
> Since unpleasant does not exist, how could
>   aversion exist?

To put this in the form of a logical reasoning: Desire and aversion have no inherent existence because their reference points, pleasant

---

30. For another analysis of how it is that things existing in mutual dependence cannot truly exist, see chapter 10, "An Examination of Fire and Firewood."

and unpleasant, do not truly exist, just as is the case with the desire and aversion that appear in dreams.

The chapter goes on to look at what are commonly known as the four mistaken views in the twenty-second verse:

> If, however, self, clean,
> Permanence, and happiness do not exist,
> Then their opposites—selfless, unclean,
> Impermanent, and suffering do not exist
>   either!

The four mistaken views are: to look at the five aggregates, which are empty of self, and see them as the self; to look at the unclean body and take it to be clean; to look at things that arise due to causes and conditions, which are impermanent, and see them as permanent; and to look at samsara, which is of the nature of suffering, and take any part of it to be happiness. Their opposites—the views of selflessness, unclean, impermanence, and suffering—are called the four correct views.

When Nagarjuna analyzes, however, he finds that neither mistaken nor correct views truly exist. For if self, clean, permanent, and happiness existed, then the views of these four would not be mistaken views after all, because when one had these views one would be focusing on things that existed, so there would not be any mistake in that. On the other hand, if these four do not exist—and their nonexistence is said to be what makes the views of them mistaken—then in fact their opposites (selfless, unclean, impermanent, and suffering) could not exist either, because they would have no reference point to depend upon for their existence. If there is no self, there can be no selflessness, because they are dependently existent; if there is no clean, there can be no unclean, because they are dependently existent; if there is no permanence, there can be no impermanence, because they are dependently existent; and if there is no happiness, there can be no suffering, because they are dependently existent. Thus, since the "correct" views' objects do not exist, the views themselves do not exist either.

Therefore, all eight of these views need to be abandoned. If we are going to posit some views as mistaken, then we have to posit all eight of these as equally mistaken. This is the ultimate view of the Middle Way, which points out that the true nature of reality transcends self, selflessness, both, and neither; transcends clean, unclean, both, and neither; transcends permanence, impermanence, both, and neither; and transcends happiness, suffering, both, and neither. That is how genuine reality is.

It is important to analyze what the true nature of mistakes really is. If we can gain certainty that essential reality transcends both being mistaken and being unmistaken, transcends both being right and being wrong, we will be able to realize that all phenomena that are opposites are really of the nature of equality. Resting within that equality, free from any mental fabrications about it, is the practice of meditative equipoise; rising up from that meditation, to view all appearances of opposites as appearance-emptiness, illusory and dreamlike, is the practice of postmeditative awareness.

24

An Examination of the Four Noble Truths

THE FOUR NOBLE TRUTHS were the Buddha's emphasis when he gave the teachings that compose the first turning of the wheel of Dharma. They present a basic outline of samsara and nirvana in terms of causes and results. The first, the truth of suffering, describes the condition that pervades every aspect and every moment of existence in samsara. Second, the truth of the origin of suffering consists of the mental afflictions and karmic actions that are samsara's causes. Third, the truth of the cessation of suffering is nirvana, the state that is the transcendence of samsara's miseries. Fourth, the truth of the path comprises the teachings and practices that are the causes of attaining the truth of cessation and thereby gaining liberation from samsara.

In the sutras of the second turning of the wheel of Dharma, however, the Buddha taught:

> Mañjushri, when you see that composite phenomena do
> not arise, you will understand suffering well.

Here the Buddha teaches that the best way to understand the truth of suffering is to know that composite phenomena do not arise and that therefore suffering does not arise either. Suffering does not really happen—it is of the nature of emptiness, as are the other three noble truths as well. To examine the four noble truths and not find anything there, to determine that they do not exist, is the stage of slight analysis. To understand that their nature is beyond all conceptual fabrications is the stage of thorough analysis.

There were people who did not understand this, however, and they criticized Nagarjuna, claiming that he was a nihilist. They said, "If your explanation of the Middle Way that refutes the inherent nature of everything were valid, there would be no four noble truths, no three rare and supreme ones (Buddha, Dharma, and Sangha), no cause and result—in fact, no conventions or expressions would exist at all." In other words, they equated emptiness with total nonexistence. In order to help them overcome their confusion, Nagarjuna composed this chapter.

Nagarjuna gives a very clear answer to these opponents' claims in the chapter's fourteenth verse:

> If emptiness is possible,
> Then everything is possible,
> But if emptiness is impossible,
> Then nothing else is possible either.

"If emptiness is possible" means "if emptiness is the true nature of things"—but what does that mean? It means that things do not *truly* exist, but rather that they exist in dependence upon the coming together of causes and conditions. Emptiness does not mean complete nothingness, it means dependent origination. Emptiness and dependent arising have the same meaning. Therefore, when emptiness is possible, everything is possible. The four noble truths, the three rare and supreme ones, and everything else in samsara and nirvana are all perfectly free to arise due to the coming together of

their causes and conditions. If things were not empty, however, if
they were not dependently arisen, then nothing would be possible.
If things truly existed, they would never change. They would have
their own nature that did not depend on causes and conditions, and
therefore causes and results would not exist. Nothing would ever
arise or cease. There could be no perception or knowledge. This is
why the four noble truths, the three rare and supreme ones, and so
forth are possible only because their nature is emptiness; they would
not be possible if they truly existed.

The eighteenth verse definitively teaches that emptiness, dependent arising, and the Middle Way all have the same meaning:

> Whatever is dependently arisen
> Is explained to be emptiness.
> Its existence is imputed in dependence
>   upon something else,
> And this is the path of the Middle Way.

The insight of the Middle Way's teachings is that whatever is
dependently arisen is empty of its own essence. The reason for this
is that whatever thing it may be, its existence is not inherent but
rather is merely imputed in dependence upon some other basis. For
example, when we look at a collection of parts and give it the name
"automobile," then "automobile" is a mere name, a mere imputation, that has no existence other than being merely that.[31] This understanding is the path of the Middle Way, free from the extremes
of existence and nonexistence, permanence and extinction, realism
and nihilism.

From among the sixteen emptinesses that the glorious Chandrakirti explains in Entering the Middle Way, the "emptiness of that
which is beyond extremes" refers to the Middle Way, emptiness,

---

31. For further explanation of how things are imputed to exist in dependence upon their
parts, see chapter 20, "An Examination of Collections."

and dependent arising. All three of these share the quality of transcending extremes. They too, however, are empty of their own nature, and that is the emptiness of that which is beyond extremes.

The nineteenth verse reads:

> There is not a single phenomenon
> That is not dependently arisen.
> Therefore, there is not a single
>   phenomenon
> That is not empty.

This verse describes the union of dependent arising and emptiness. Emptiness pervades all dependently arisen phenomena, and from within emptiness, the great variety of dependently arisen appearances manifest.

Since it is the case that everything included in the four noble truths is dependently arisen, the four noble truths are empty. Since it is the case that everything in samsara and nirvana is dependently arisen, everything in samsara and nirvana is empty.

Since it is the case that every single thing that appears in a dream is dependently arisen, everything in the dream is empty.

Similarly, since it is the case that all inner and outer phenomena are dependently arisen mere appearances, there is not a single one of them, either on the inside or on the outside, that is not empty.

As we saw earlier, Milarepa also sang about the union of dependent arising and emptiness in his *Song of the Profound Definitive Meaning Sung on the Snowy Range*:

> When you're sure that conduct's work is
>   luminous light,
> And you're sure that interdependence is
>   emptiness,

A doer and deed refined until they're
   gone—
This way of working with conduct, it works
   quite well!

Thus we can see that the conclusions that the noble Nagarjuna comes to through logical analysis and those that the lord of yogis Milarepa realizes with wisdom arising from meditation are exactly the same. This should help us to gain certainty in both of these great masters' teachings.

25

An Examination
of Nirvana

In the *Prajñāpāramitā Sutras*, the Buddha taught:
Nirvana, too, is just like a dream.

❊ ❊ ❊ ❊ ❊

NAGARJUNA COMPOSED THIS CHAPTER in answer to those who argued, "If everything is empty, how could there be any nirvana, the 'transcendence of suffering'? If the things that compose samsara—the aggregates, mental afflictions, and karmic actions—do not exist in the first place, how could there be any transcendence of them? In fact, nirvana does exist, and therefore the samsara that it transcends must also exist. The aggregates, mental afflictions, and karmic actions all exist, because the arhats who achieve their cessation exist, and the arhats exist because the nirvana they attain exists." Thus, in order to help these people correct their mistaken belief in the true existence of things, Nagarjuna presents an analysis of nirvana and proves that it too is empty of its own essence.

The Buddha taught about nirvana in different ways, depending on the needs of his disciples. To those who were weary of samsara's suffering, who were depressed by it, the Buddha taught about nirvana as if it truly existed. To them he described nirvana as the genuine and irreversible liberation from samsara, the peace that was the cessation of samsara's suffering. Now that those people had hope that there was in fact a way they could gain freedom from samsara's misery, they were filled with longing to attain it, so they renounced samsara and became eager entrants into the path of Dharma. Then, however, to his disciples who were fixated on the idea that nirvana was real, the Buddha taught that nirvana does not inherently exist after all, that it too is just like a dream. Finally, to his most apt disciples, the Buddha described the true nature of nirvana, which, like the nature of all other phenomena, cannot be described as being existent or nonexistent because it is beyond all conceptual fabrications.

Thus, the way that the stages of the teachings proceed is as follows: First, it must be explained that samsara is of the nature of suffering, because if one is still distracted by the thought that one can get some happiness out of this existence, one will not think about the Dharma. Therefore, it first must be taught that everything in existence is of the nature of suffering. Then, when that thought of everything in existence being of the nature of suffering gets really depressing, one is introduced to the concept of nirvana and is taught that the possibility of liberation from this suffering exists. This eases one's sadness and gives one great incentive to practice the Dharma with the goal of attaining nirvana's peace. However, there is still this thought that nirvana is something real, and if one does not free oneself from that, one will never be able to attain nirvana. Therefore, one is then taught that nirvana does not truly exist, that it has no inherent nature. Finally, what remains is this clinging to nirvana being nonexistent, which also is an obscuration to one's wisdom. In order to be free from that, one is taught that the nature of nirvana transcends both existence and nonexistence, and that this is the ultimate description of genuine reality.

Since Nagarjuna is responding to criticism from those who believe that nirvana truly exists, he must begin with the second stage and demonstrate that nirvana is empty of inherent nature. One way he does this is by asking, "If nirvana exists, then does it exist before the suffering of samsara that it transcends, or after it? Which one of these comes first?"

Nirvana could not exist before samsara's suffering, because if it did, what suffering would it transcend? There would be no meaning to nirvana's defining characteristics of being the transcendence of suffering if that were the case.

Samsara could not exist before nirvana either, because if it did, then the transcendence of suffering would be a newly created thing, a fabricated entity, subject to the same decay as every other thing that arises anew. Attaining nirvana would not guarantee permanent liberation from samsara, because nirvana would eventually decay just like everything else. The naturally present nirvana would not be the basic nature of reality that the Buddha described it to be.[32] Furthermore, if samsara existed before nirvana, and thus nirvana arose after samsara ceased, what would there be in between the two? Samsara's suffering would stop, then there would be a gap that would be neither samsara nor nirvana, then nirvana would arise from out of that nothingness without a cause.

Samsara and nirvana cannot exist simultaneously either, for all the reasons presented in earlier chapters that negate the possibility that two dependent phenomena could truly exist simultaneously. Furthermore, if you think about it from the perspective of the continuum of one individual's existence, how could samsara and nirvana both be present in one individual's mindstream at the same

---

32. "Naturally present nirvana" is a synonym for the dharmakaya of natural purity. See note 28, page 145.

time? It would be impossible for one individual to both suffer and transcend suffering simultaneously.

Thus runs the logical proof of nirvana's emptiness of true existence. If one asks, "Well, then what is the nature of nirvana after all?" Nagarjuna describes it in the third verse:

> Nothing to abandon, nothing to attain,
> Nothing extinct, nothing permanent,
> No cessation, no arising—
> This is how nirvana is taught to be.

In the abiding nature of reality, there are no mental afflictions to begin with, and therefore there is nothing to abandon—there is nothing flawed that needs to be gotten rid of or removed. There are also no qualities of nirvana that somehow first do not exist and then later need to be created or attained. Furthermore, the continuum of an individual's aggregates does not become extinct at the point of nirvana, nor does it remain in a permanent, unchanging state. Finally, nothing existent ceases and nothing nonexistent arises. This is essential reality, dharmata, and this is precisely how nirvana is taught to be. In short, it is dharmadhatu, the expanse of genuine reality, beyond abandonment and attainment, extinction and permanence, and arising and ceasing. This is the natural nirvana, the nirvana that is the true nature of reality, the essence of all the infinite phenomena that appear. This natural nirvana is different from the nirvana that one achieves at the time of enlightenment, when even one's most subtle obscurations are purified and one's realization of the natural nirvana becomes completely perfect. That is called "nirvana free of fleeting stains." At the time of enlightenment, the Buddha is said to be endowed with two types of purity: naturally present purity and the purity of being free from fleeting stains. In this verse, it is the first of these two that is emphasized.[33]

---

33. For a similar discussion of the two types of dharmakaya that parallel the two types of nirvana, see note 28, page 145.

The *Heart of Wisdom Sutra* teaches:

All phenomena are emptiness: They have no characteristics, no birth, no cessation, no stains, no freedom from stains, no decrease, and no increase.

The meaning of this third verse and that of this passage from the sutra are the same. Furthermore, Nagarjuna's verse describes how nirvana is free from all extremes, and so it is very important. You should definitely memorize it.

In his song *Eight Ornaments of the Profound Meaning*, Milarepa sang:

To bring one's thoughts to the point of
their exhaustion,
Is this not buddhahood gained in a single
life?

This is also in harmony with what Nagarjuna is teaching here. Perfect realization of reality beyond extremes means that all concepts of those extremes utterly cease. That is how it is described, but at the same time, since thoughts have no inherent nature in the first place, there is no real cessation of them either.

The nineteenth verse describes how samsara and nirvana are actually undifferentiable:

Samsara is not the slightest bit different
from nirvana.
Nirvana is not the slightest bit different
from samsara.

From the perspective of precise knowledge analyzing the nature of genuine reality, once the true existence of nirvana is refuted, then one realizes that there is no samsara that is even the slightest bit different from nirvana, and no nirvana that is even the slightest bit different from samsara. In short, samsara and nirvana are of the nature of equality, because both have a nature beyond all conceptual fabrications about what it might be, and because both in their true nature are originally pure.

As the Fifth Karmapa Deshin Shekpa states:

> Whatever is the suchness of samsara, that is nirvana.

Thus, there is no difference between the suchness of samsara and the suchness of nirvana. Samsara and nirvana are therefore equality. There is no difference between them in the true nature of reality.

In the Mahayana sutras, the Buddha taught the ten types of equality—the ten ways in which all things are essentially the same. The ultimate meaning of all of them, what they all point to, is the equality of samsara and nirvana.

For this reason, the twentieth verse states:

> The true nature of nirvana
> Is the true nature of samsara,
> And between these two
> There is not even the tiniest, subtlest
>   difference.

The essential reality of samsara is the essential reality of nirvana, and in this essential reality, there is not even the slightest difference between them. Samsara and nirvana are equality.

The great siddha Dombi Heruka sang:

> Existence and peace are equality,
> Free from all conceptuality,
> So striving and straining to accomplish
>   some goal—
> Oh, what a tiring thing to do!

Body and mind, nonduality—
Spacious and relaxed transparency.
To think that body and mind are two
    different things
Is a neurotic, crazy, afflicted thing to do!

Self and other not two in dharmakaya,
To cling to good and bad—I pity the fool!

These verses teach of the equality of samsaric existence and nirvanic peace, the equality of body and mind, and the equality of self and other.

You can have a dream of being bound in iron chains and then being set free. When you do not know you are dreaming, these two states seem to be different: Being bound in chains is bad, being set free from them is good, and they both seem to be real. When you know that you are dreaming, you know that both are mere appearances. In the abiding nature of reality, the bondage and the liberation are equality—between the true nature of bondage and the true nature of liberation, there is not the slightest difference. This is how you should understand it.

Therefore, happiness and suffering are just the way things appear to be. The way things really are is that happiness and suffering are equality. In his vajra song of realization, *The Eight Types of Nonduality*, Gyalwa Gotsangpa sang:

Complete happiness and comfort and
Overwhelming pain and suffering
These distinctions don't exist in the pure
    expanse—
So! How joyful! How happy! Sudden
    victory!

The equality of samsara and nirvana is also an integral part of the view of Dzogchen. In his commentary, Ju Mipham Rinpoche describes from his own personal experience how it is that one must rely on Nagarjuna's reasonings in order to realize Dzogchen's view:

> In the infinite expanse of equality without reference point, all the phenomena of samsara and nirvana are perfectly complete—this is the supreme vehicle's profound view of Dzogchen. Thanks to the noble Nagarjuna's king of reasonings, the light of wisdom's brilliant flame shone upon me, dispelling the darkness of doubts and causing profound certainty to arise. Ema! A la la! How wonderful! How blissful!

Furthermore, since one must rely on Nagarjuna's reasonings in order to realize the essence of Dzogchen, it is the same for Mahamudra. Those who studied at the *shedra*s (philosophical universities) in Tibet studied *The Fundamental Wisdom of the Middle Way* and Chandrakirti's *Entering the Middle Way* and other similar texts over the course of many years. Mahamudra and Dzogchen were not studied, however, because it is the Middle Way texts that are filled with such a vast array of different arguments and logical reasonings that one can pursue the study of them in a manner that is both subtle and profound.

In the Mahamudra teachings as well, we find statements such as this one from Karmapa Rangjung Dorje's *Mahamudra Aspiration Prayer*:

> As for mind, there is no mind! Mind is empty of essence.

If you gain certainty in mind's emptiness of essence by analyzing it with the reasoning that refutes arising from the four extremes and with others as well, then your understanding of Mahamudra will become profound. Otherwise, you could recite this line, but in your mind it would be nothing more than an opinion or a guess. The eleventh verse in the *Mahamudra Aspiration Prayer* reads:

It is not existent—even the Victorious Ones
 do not see it,
It is not nonexistent—it is the basis of all
 samsara and nirvana,
It is not the contradiction of being both—it
 is the Middle Way path of union—
May we realize mind's essential reality, free
 from extremes.

Here as well, to understand this refutation of the extremes of existence and nonexistence with regard to the mind, one needs to have a good understanding of Nagarjuna's reasonings, for example, the reasonings behind this verse from chapter 22, "An Examination of the Tathagata":

The Tathagata cannot be called "empty,"
 nor "not empty," nor both, nor neither.
Use these terms as conventional
 designations.[34]

Once one has analyzed using logical reasoning, it is impossible to assert anything about the true nature of reality. When we describe conventional appearances, however, the use of terms and designations is appropriate.

If you study these reasonings presented in *The Fundamental Wisdom of the Middle Way*, when you receive Mahamudra and Dzogchen explanations of emptiness and lack of inherent reality, you will already be familiar with what is being taught and so you will not need to learn anything new.

Mipham Rinpoche composed a brief text called *The Beacon of Certainty*, in which he states:

---

34. Verse 11.

In order to have perfect certainty in alpha-
    purity,
One must have perfect understanding of
    the view of the Consequence school.

Alpha-purity, or original, primordial purity, is the view of Dzogchen, and in order to perfect that view, one must perfect one's understanding of the Middle Way Consequence school's view. What
this implies is that the view of alpha-purity and the view of the
Consequence school are the same.

26

An Examination of
the Twelve Links
of Existence

In the sutras, the Buddha taught:

That which is dependently arisen does not arise, and therefore
it is dependently arisen.

❋ ❋ ❋ ❋ ❋

IN THIS WAY, THE BUDDHA EXPLAINED that whatever arises due
to the coming together of causes and conditions does not truly arise.
Therefore, it is dependently arisen, meaning that its arising is just a
mere appearance. This characteristic of dependent arising is important to remember: When something is *dependently* arisen, it is not
truly arisen. It is like a water-moon. Due to the coming together of
causes and conditions, the moon appears on the surface of the
water, but in fact no moon has arisen there at all.

There are several different explanations for why this chapter was written. The commentary entitled *Completely Fearless*[35] and the master Buddhapalita[36] both assert that the followers of the Shravakayana asked Nagarjuna, "You have explained how to realize genuine reality according to the Mahayana tradition. Now, please teach us how to enter genuine reality according to the Shravaka tradition." In other words, in the first twenty-five chapters, Nagarjuna explained how to follow the Mahayana path, and now, followers of the Shravakayana asked him for teachings on the path they had chosen to follow.

Bhavaviveka[37] writes that there were those who argued, "Nagarjuna, earlier in the text you wrote, 'The Buddha did not teach any Dharma to anyone.'[38] Did not the Buddha, though, teach about the twelve dependently arisen links of existence?" In response, Nagarjuna composed this chapter to explain that the Buddha did not give any truly existent teachings, and thus he did not teach that the twelve links exist in essence, but rather that they are mere appearances.

Finally, Chandrakirti explains that there were those who said, "Samsara exists because its cause, the twelve links of existence, exists, and nirvana exists because its cause, the reversal of those twelve links, exists. Furthermore, if samsara and nirvana were not two different things, why would they appear to be so? If existence and peace were not two different things, why would the terms *existence* and *peace* exist?" Thus, in order to explain how it is that phenomena do not exist at the same time they appear, how it is that phenomena are only dependently arisen, Nagarjuna composed this chapter.

Indian scholars composed a great number of commentaries on

---

35. It is not certain who authored this particular commentary. Some say that it was composed by Nagarjuna himself, but others deny this.

36. Buddhapalita wrote one of the first commentaries on *The Fundamental Wisdom of the Middle Way*, from the perspective of the Middle Way Consequence school's view.

37. Bhavaviveka followed Buddhapalita and composed a commentary on *The Fundamental Wisdom of the Middle Way* from the perspective of the Middle Way Autonomy school's view.

38. Chapter 25, verse 24 (not included here).

The Fundamental Wisdom of the Middle Way, but from among them all, the four quoted above are the most important. In Tibet, scholars from the four main lineages of Sakya, Gelug, Kagyü, and Nyingma composed their own commentaries to the text. Of all of these, the most extensive is probably Je Tsong-khapa's *Great Commentary on the Fundamental Wisdom of the Middle Way, Called "An Ocean of Reasoning,"* which Tsong-khapa composed while residing in a cave in the hills above Sera Monastery.[39]

The twelve links of existence are the stages sentient beings continually pass through, life after life, as they wander without respite through the three higher and three lower realms of samsara. The first nine verses in this chapter describe the twelve links in their "forward progression": how one link in this samsaric chain gives rise to the next. The last three verses describe the "reverse progression": how those who have realized selflessness are able to root out the cause of the twelve links and gain liberation from samsara.

To summarize the forward progression of the twelve links, the first link in the chain and the source of all the others is *ignorance* of the basic nature of reality. This ignorance obscures the mind and as a result one believes that the self of the individual truly exists. This causes one to perform *karmic action* (2), either virtuous, unvirtuous, or neutral; and after one's present life has ended, it causes rebirth in one of the higher or lower realms of samsara.

This samsaric rebirth begins as one's *consciousness* (3) finds its way to the place where it will begin its next life; in the case of humans, for example, in the womb of the mother. Immediately upon entering the mother's womb at the moment of conception, consciousness joins with the very first stages of the material body, and thus begins the stage of *name and form* (4). "Name" refers to the four mental aggregates that cannot be physically perceived, namely feelings, discriminations, formations, and consciousnesses, and

---

39. Tsong-khapa (1357–1419) was the founder of the Gelugpa lineage of Tibetan Buddhism.

"form" refers to the aggregate of the same name, the sentient being's new physical body.

Shortly thereafter, the five sense faculties and the mental faculty develop, and this constitutes the stage of the six inner *sources of consciousness* (5). This enables the stage of *contact* (6) with the six objects—sights, sounds, odors, tastes, tactile sensations, and phenomena. Contact with different objects gives rise to *feelings* (7), either pleasant, unpleasant, or neutral, depending on what the particular object is. These feelings give rise to *craving* (8), which is the desire for pleasant contact to occur and unpleasant contact to remain absent. When this craving intensifies, it becomes *grasping* (9), which has four specific types: grasping at sense pleasures, at wrong views, at one's own conduct as supreme, and at the belief in a self, at constant thoughts of "I," "me," and "mine."

Grasping's intensity causes one to perform defiled karmic actions with body, speech, and mind—this is *existence* (10). This leads once again to *birth* (11) in samsara, followed by *aging and death* (12), and then the process begins all over again, in an uninterrupted cycle of suffering that Nagarjuna describes in the eighth and ninth verses:

> "Existence" is karmic action performed
>   with the five aggregates.
> From existence comes birth,
> And from birth,
> Aging, death, agony, bewailing, pain,
>   unhappiness, and agitation come
>   without fail.
> Thus, the only thing born
> Is a massive heap of suffering.

When one performs karmic actions with body, speech, and mind, that is the cause of future birth. All who are born must experience aging and the agony of being separated from what pleases them, an agony that becomes most intense when they are dying. Wretchedly they cry out, bewailing their torment. "Pain" refers to physical harm experienced by the five sense faculties and "unhappiness" to exclusively mental suffering, both of which continuously agitate the mind. Thus, the only thing that takes birth in samsara is a massive heap of suffering.

Thus is the pathetic state in which sentient beings find themselves. However, when Nagarjuna states, "The *only* thing born is a massive heap of suffering," he means that no truly existent self is born along with the suffering. The suffering that is born is therefore only a mere appearance, arisen due to the coming together of causes and conditions. It is not real because no self to experience it actually exists. If the suffering were real, we could never gain liberation from it; it would be our permanent nature. Since it is only a mere appearance, however, it comes to an end when the causes and conditions responsible for it are no longer produced. As the tenth verse explains:

> The root of samsara is karmic action.
> Therefore, the wise do not perform it.
> Therefore, the ones who commit karmic
> acts are the unwise,
> Not the wise, because they see the precise
> nature.

Those who are endowed with the wisdom that realizes selflessness, the precise nature of reality, do not perform defiled karmic actions, the causes of samsaric rebirth. They are able to refrain from committing karmic actions not simply because they choose to do so, however, but rather because they have completely eradicated the ignorance that is karmic actions' cause. As the eleventh verse explains:

> When ignorance ceases,
> Karmic actions cease.

The cessation of ignorance
Is the result of meditating with knowledge
    of reality's precise nature.

When ignorance of selflessness ceases, the reverse progression of
the twelve links takes effect. As ignorance is the root cause of the
next eleven links, when it ceases, so does samsara, never to arise
again. This wonderful process is summarized in the twelfth and final
verse:

When the earlier links cease,
The later links do not occur,
And that which is only a heap of suffering
Perfectly comes to an end.

So the story has a happy ending after all!

By the end of the first twenty-five chapters of the text, Nagarjuna
had successfully refuted all the claims of the followers of the Shravakayana who asserted that things truly exist. At that point, with all of
their arguments discredited, some of these followers of the Shravakayana gained enthusiasm for the teachings on emptiness and entered the Mahayana path. Others did not, however, and remained
where they were, crestfallen. Seeing the state they were in, Nagarjuna
explained the forward and reverse progressions of the twelve links
of existence in a manner that was in harmony with their own tradition. This made them happy, and it also better prepared them to
understand how extraordinary the Mahayana's presentation of
emptiness actually is.

27

An Examination of Views

In the sutras, the Buddha taught:

The ones who correctly see dependent arising just as it is will not adhere to views of an earlier, present, or future period of time.

❖ ❖ ❖ ❖ ❖

IT IS POSSIBLE to have one of several different views about the self and the universe it inhabits. For example, one could believe that the self and the universe always existed in the past, or that at some point in the past they did not exist. One could believe that the self and the universe will always exist in the future, or that at some point they will not. Finally, one could hold the view that they exist now or that they do not.

Those who see dependent arising just as it is, however, do not adhere to any such views. They know that the true nature of the self and the universe transcends all such notions of existence and nonexistence. They know that when things appear either to exist or not to exist, it is only mere appearance manifesting due to the coming together of causes and conditions, with no inherent nature to it at all. This is the meaning of the Buddha's teaching quoted above, and in this chapter Nagarjuna proves the validity of this teaching with logical reasoning.

Here again, there are different explanations given for why this chapter was written. The commentary entitled *Completely Fearless* and Buddhapalita both assert that followers of the Shravakayana asked Nagarjuna, "Please explain how it is that all the different permutations of views are impossible from the perspective of the Shravakayana sutras as well," and that Nagarjuna composed this chapter to fulfill their request.

Bhavaviveka writes that there were those who argued, "The five aggregates exist because they are the support in which views abide," and that in response Nagarjuna wrote this chapter to explain how it is that views themselves do not exist.

Finally, Chandrakirti states that Nagarjuna composed this chapter in answer to those who asked him, "The Buddha taught, 'The ones who see dependent arising will not believe in an earlier or later period of time.' What are these earlier and later periods of time, and how can one come to abandon the belief in their existence?"

By analyzing the true nature of the self and the universe, we can gain certainty that none of the views that hold them to be permanent, impermanent, finite, or infinite are accurate. As Nagarjuna teaches in the twenty-second verse:

> The continuum of the aggregates
> Is like the continuum of a butter lamp.
> Therefore, to say that the aggregates are
>   finite is illogical
> And to say that they are infinite is illogical.

Individuals are composed of the five aggregates. The continuum of these five aggregates that spans the course of countless past and future lifetimes is like the continuum of a butter lamp, and therefore it cannot be described as finite or infinite. Like a butter lamp, the past aggregates have all ceased to exist, which eliminates the possibility that anything within them has infinite duration. That the future moments of the aggregates unfailingly occur, however, eliminates the possibility that they are finite, that they have some time limit to their existence.

Here it is also helpful to consider one's aggregates that appear in a dream: They are neither finite nor infinite, because they are just dependently arisen mere appearances.

The twenty-ninth and final verse of the chapter is a summary of all the refutations of the various views that have been explained up to this point:

> Since all things are empty,
> Why would anyone, anywhere, at any time,
> View things as being permanent or
>   anything else?

The commentary to this verse reads, "The genuine nature of reality transcends all conceptual fabrications. Therefore, all inner and outer things are dependently arisen and empty, like reflections, so why would anyone who knew this, anywhere, at any time, view things as being permanent or anything else? They would not, because they would know everything to be emptiness."

There is no valid reason for the views that things are permanent, impermanent, finite, or infinite to arise, because all phenomena are dependently arisen, like reflections, and because the nature of reality is the emptiness that transcends conceptual fabrications. Phenomena are of this nature of emptiness because their mode of appearance is that they are dependently arisen mere appearances.

This chapter has demonstrated that these inferior views of permanence and so forth do not truly exist, and therefore the one who holds them does not really exist either. The explanation that some views are inferior can be made only in dependence upon the notion that there are some better views to have—therefore, this is only a presentation from the perspective of apparent reality and the concepts that fabricate it. In the true nature of reality, there are neither good views nor bad ones. Samsara and nirvana are of the nature of perfect equality; they are undifferentiable. As Nagarjuna taught in chapter 25, "An Examination of Nirvana":

> Samsara is not the slightest bit different
>   from nirvana.
> Nirvana is not the slightest bit different
>   from samsara.[40]

> The true nature of nirvana
> Is the true nature of samsara,
> And between these two
> There is not even the tiniest, subtlest
>   difference.[41]

Therefore, there are really no inferior views, nor anyone who has inferior views. These things simply do not exist in genuine reality. Nagarjuna described the way that things are imagined and designated in apparent reality in this verse from chapter 7, "An Examination of the Composite":

> Like a dream, like an illusion,
> Like a city of gandharvas,
> That's how birth and that's how living,
> That's how dying are taught to be.[42]

---

40. Verse 19.
41. Verse 20.
42. Verse 34.

Concluding Homage

Holding us in your incredible wisdom and love,
You taught us the genuine Dharma
To help us abandon all views.
I prostrate before you, Gautama.

❖ ❖ ❖ ❖ ❖

THIS IS THE HOMAGE with which Nagarjuna concludes the text, offering his prostration to the Buddha in gratitude for the Buddha's tremendous kindness.

The commentary to this verse reads, "The Protector of Beings taught the genuine Dharma not out of any desire for wealth, respect, or renown, but rather out of his completely pure wisdom and great compassion imbued with nonreferential love.[43] Holding the beings who wander in samsara close to his heart, he taught the genuine Dharma in order to help them abandon all inferior views that cling

---

43. The Buddha's nonreferential love is the perfect union of love and emptiness. It is completely free of the concepts of subject, object, and action; at the same time it spontaneously performs limitless benefit for sentient beings without any notion of some being more worthy of affection than others. It is the very essence of the Buddha's enlightened mind, and manifesting it within oneself is the ultimate fruition of the Mahayana path.

to mistaken extremes. His teachings are the cause of attaining the omniscient wisdom that abides neither in the extreme of existence nor in that of peace. . . . They are prajñāpāramitā, the teachings on dependent arising that completely dissolve all conceptual fabrications. You who taught in this way are the sage called Gautama, the unequaled Lion of the Shakyas. Recalling your great kindness, and with deep respect, I prostrate before you." Thus ends *The Fundamental Wisdom of the Middle Way.*

Appendix 1

Root Verses from *The Fundamental Wisdom of the Middle Way*

Opening homage
I prostrate to the one
Who teaches that whatever is dependently arisen
Does not arise, does not cease,
Is not permanent, is not extinct,
Does not come, does not go,
And is neither one thing nor different things.
I prostrate to the perfect Buddha, the supreme of all who speak,
Who completely dissolves all fabrications and teaches peace.

Chapter 1: an examination of causal conditions
Not from self, not from other,
Not from both, nor without cause:
Things do not arise
At any place, at any time. (1)[44]

Chapter 2: an examination of coming and going
On the path that has been traveled, there is no moving,
On the path that has not been traveled, there is no moving either,
And in some other place besides the path that has been traveled
    and the path that has not,
Motions are not perceptible in any way at all. (1)

---

44. Numbers in parentheses refer to the numbers of the root verses in the specific chapters.

Chapter 3: an examination of the sources of consciousness

Know that these reasonings refuting the faculty that sees
Refute the faculties that hear, smell, taste, touch, and the mental
    faculty as well,
Refute the hearer and the other perceiving consciousnesses,
Refute sound and the other perceived objects. (8)

Chapter 4: an examination of the aggregates

Except for there being the cause of form,
Form would not be seen.
Except for there being what we call "form,"
The cause of form would not appear either. (1)

Feelings, discriminations, formations,
Minds, and all the things there are
Are susceptible to the same stages of analysis
That forms have been put through here. (7)

When emptiness comes up for debate,
Whatever answers try to prove true existence,
Those answers are unsound
Because they are equivalent to the very thesis to be proved. (8)

When explanations are given about emptiness,
Whoever would try to find faults in them
Will not be able to find any faults at all,
Because the faults are equivalent to the very thesis to be proved. (9)

Chapter 5: an examination of the elements

Space can in no way exist
Prior to its defining characteristics.
If space existed prior to its defining characteristics,
It would follow that space could exist without defining
    characteristics. (1)

Therefore, space is not something, it is not nothing,
It is not a basis for characteristics, its defining characteristics do
   not exist,
And the other five elements are precisely the same. (7)

Those with little intelligence
View things as being existent or nonexistent.
They do not see that what is to be seen
Is perfect and utter peace. (8)

CHAPTER 6: AN EXAMINATION OF DESIRE AND THE DESIROUS ONE

If before desire existed,
If without any desire there existed a desirous one,
In dependence upon that, there would in fact be desire,
For when there is a desirous one, there is also desire. (1)

CHAPTER 7: AN EXAMINATION OF THE COMPOSITE

Arising, abiding, and ceasing do not exist,
And therefore there are no composite things.
Since composite things are utterly nonexistent,
How could anything noncomposite exist? (33)

Like a dream, like an illusion,
Like a city of gandharvas,
That's how birth and that's how living,
That's how dying are taught to be. (34)

CHAPTER 8: AN EXAMINATION OF ACTORS AND ACTIONS

An actor exists in dependence upon an action,
An action exists in dependence upon an actor,
And apart from that,
No reason for their existence can be seen. (12)

CHAPTER 9: AN EXAMINATION OF WHAT COMES FIRST

The one who experiences perceptions does not exist
Before, during, or after the experiences of seeing and so forth.

Knowing this, all thoughts of an experiencer of perceptions either
existing or not existing are reversed. (12)

CHAPTER 10: AN EXAMINATION OF FIRE
AND FIREWOOD

If something exists in dependence upon something else,
But that thing upon which it depends
Must also depend upon it,
Then which one of these exists in dependence upon which? (10)

The firewood itself is not the fire,
There is no fire that exists apart from the firewood,
The fire does not possess the firewood,
The fire does not support the firewood, and the firewood does
not support the fire. (14)

This examination of fire and firewood
Refutes the self and the aggregates it appropriates in all five ways.
Similarly, examining vases, blankets, and so forth,
It is perfectly explained that none of them exist in any of these
five ways. (15)

CHAPTER 11: AN EXAMINATION OF SAMSARA

Since one cannot happen before the others,
And they cannot happen simultaneously,
Why would you ever think
That birth, aging, and death truly exist? (6)

CHAPTER 12: AN EXAMINATION OF SUFFERING

That which is only suffering does not arise
From any of the four extremes, and not only that,
All outer phenomena do not arise
From any of the four extremes either. (10)

CHAPTER 13: AN EXAMINATION OF THE PRECISE
NATURE OF REALITY

If there were the slightest thing not empty,
There would be that much emptiness existent.

Since, however, there is not the slightest thing not empty,
How could emptiness exist? (7)

CHAPTER 14: AN EXAMINATION OF CONTACT

The object seen, the eye that sees, and the seer—
These three do not meet each other,
Either in pairs or all together. (1)

Desire, the desirous one, and the object of desire do not meet
either,
Nor do any of the remaining afflictions,
Nor any of the remaining sources of consciousness:
In these sets of three there is neither meeting in pairs nor all
together. (2)

CHAPTER 15: AN EXAMINATION OF THINGS AND THE ABSENCE OF THINGS

In his *Pith Instructions to Katyayana,*
The one who knows all things and all absences of things,
The Transcendent Conqueror,
Refuted both existence and nonexistence. (7)

"Existence" is the view of permanence,
"Nonexistence" is the view of extinction,
Therefore, the wise do not abide
Either in existence or in nonexistence. (10)

CHAPTER 16: AN EXAMINATION OF BONDAGE AND LIBERATION

If one asks, "Do the aggregates wander?"
No, they do not, because permanent aggregates could not
wander,
And impermanent aggregates could not wander either.
The same holds true for sentient beings. (1)

If the individual really wandered from one existence to the next,
Then in between existences, there would be no existence!

With no existence and no appropriated aggregates,
What individual could possibly be wandering? (3)

No matter how they might be,
It would be untenable for the aggregates to attain nirvana.
No matter how they might be,
It would be untenable for sentient beings to attain nirvana. (4)

The aggregates, characterized by birth and decay,
Are not bound and do not become free.
Similarly, sentient beings
Are not bound and do not become free. (5)

Do the mental afflictions bind?
They do not bind one already afflicted,
And they do not bind one who is not afflicted,
So when do they have the opportunity to bind anyone? (6)

There is no nirvana to be produced
And no samsara to be cleared away.
In essential reality, what samsara is there?
What is there that can be called nirvana? (10)

Chapter 17: an examination of karmic actions and results

Mental afflictions, actions, and bodies,
As well as actors and results,
Are like cities of gandharvas,
Like mirages, and like dreams. (33)

Chapter 18: an examination of self and phenomena

If the self were the aggregates,
It would be something that arises and ceases.
If the self were something other than the aggregates,
It would not have the aggregates' characteristics. (1)

If there is no "me" in the first place,
How could there be anything that belongs to me?

When "me" and "mine" are found to be peace,
Clinging to "me" and "mine" ceases. (2)

The ones who do not cling to "me" or "mine"
Do not exist either.
Those who do not cling to "me" or "mine" see accurately,
So they do not see a self. (3)

When one stops thinking of the inner and outer aggregates as
   being "me" or "mine"
All wrong views disappear,
And once they have disappeared, birth in the cycle of existence
   stops. (4)

When karmic actions and mental afflictions cease, that is
   liberation. (5a)

Unknowable by analogy; peace;
Not of the fabric of fabrications;
Nonconceptual; free of distinctions—
These are the characteristics of the precise nature. (9)

CHAPTER 19: AN EXAMINATION OF TIME
If the present and the future depended on the past,
The present and the future would exist in the past.(1)

CHAPTER 20: AN EXAMINATION OF COLLECTIONS
If cause and result were one,
Then producer and produced would be the same thing.
If cause and result were different,
Then causes and noncauses would be equivalent. (19)

CHAPTER 21: AN EXAMINATION OF EMERGENCE
AND DECAY
Emergence and decay
Cannot logically be the same thing.
Emergence and decay
Cannot logically be different things. (10)

When you think you see emergence and decay,
It is only bewilderment that sees emergence and decay. (11)

CHAPTER 22: AN EXAMINATION OF THE TATHAGATA

The Tathagata cannot be called "empty," nor "not empty," nor
    both, nor neither.
Use these terms as mere conventional designations. (11)

Permanent, impermanent, and so forth, the four—
Where are they in this peace?
Finite, infinite, and so forth, the four—
Where are they in this peace? (12)

Whatever is the nature of the Tathagata,
That is the nature of wandering beings.
The Tathagata has no inherent nature;
Wandering beings have no inherent nature. (16)

CHAPTER 23: AN EXAMINATION OF MISTAKES

How could it be possible for
Sentient beings who are like illusions
Or objects that are like reflections
To be either pleasant or unpleasant? (9)

We imagine something to be pleasant
Based on our idea of what is unpleasant.
But unpleasant too does not exist independent of pleasant.
Therefore, for pleasant to truly exist would be impossible. (10)

We imagine something to be unpleasant
Based on our idea of what is pleasant.
But pleasant too does not exist independent of unpleasant.
Therefore, for unpleasant to truly exist would be impossible. (11)

Since pleasant does not exist, how could desire exist?
Since unpleasant does not exist, how could aversion exist? (12)

If, however, self, clean,
Permanence, and happiness do not exist,

Then their opposites—selfless, unclean,
Impermanent, and suffering do not exist either! (22)

CHAPTER 24: AN EXAMINATION OF THE FOUR NOBLE TRUTHS

If emptiness is possible,
Then everything is possible,
But if emptiness is impossible,
Then nothing else is possible either. (14)

Whatever is dependently arisen
Is explained to be emptiness.
Its existence is imputed in dependence upon something else,
And this is the path of the Middle Way. (18)

There is not a single phenomenon
That is not dependently arisen.
Therefore, there is not a single phenomenon
That is not empty. (19)

CHAPTER 25: AN EXAMINATION OF NIRVANA

Nothing to abandon, nothing to attain,
Nothing extinct, nothing permanent,
No cessation, no arising—
This is how nirvana is taught to be. (3)

Samsara is not the slightest bit different from nirvana.
Nirvana is not the slightest bit different from samsara. (19)

The true nature of nirvana
Is the true nature of samsara,
And between these two
There is not even the tiniest, subtlest difference. (20)

CHAPTER 26: AN EXAMINATION OF THE TWELVE LINKS OF EXISTENCE

"Existence" is karmic action performed with the five aggregates.
From existence comes birth,

And from birth,
Aging, death, agony, bewailing, pain, unhappiness, and agitation
 come without fail.
Thus, the only thing born
Is a massive heap of suffering. (8–9)

The root of samsara is karmic action.
Therefore, the wise do not perform it.
Therefore, the ones who commit karmic acts are the unwise,
Not the wise, because they see the precise nature. (10)

When ignorance ceases,
Karmic actions cease.
The cessation of ignorance
Is the result of meditating with knowledge of reality's precise
 nature. (11)

When the earlier links cease,
The later links do not occur,
And that which is only a heap of suffering
Perfectly comes to an end. (12)

Chapter 27: an examination of views

The continuum of the aggregates
Is like the continuum of a butter lamp.
Therefore, to say that the aggregates are finite is illogical
And to say that they are infinite is illogical. (22)

Since all things are empty,
Why would anyone, anywhere, at any time,
View things as being permanent or anything else? (29)

Concluding homage

Holding us in your incredible wisdom and love,
You taught us the genuine Dharma
To help us abandon all views.
I prostrate before you, Gautama.

Appendix 2

The *Heart of Wisdom Sutra*

In Sanskrit: *Bhagavati prajña paramita hridaya*. In Tibetan: *Jom den dema sherab gyi parol tu chin pay nying po*. (In English: "Noble Lady, Transcendent Conqueror, Heart of Transcendent Wisdom.")

Homage to the Noble Lady, Transcendent Conqueror, Heart of Transcendent Wisdom.

Thus I have heard. Once the Transcendent Conqueror[45] was dwelling in Rajghir on Vulture Peak, together with a great sangha of bhikshus[46] and a great sangha of bodhisattvas. At that time, from among the different Dharmas, the Transcendent Conqueror entered the samadhi called "Profound Illumination."

At the same time the noble and powerful Avalokiteshvara, the bodhisattva-mahasattva, looked clearly at the profound practice of transcendent wisdom and saw clearly that the five aggregates are empty by nature.

Then by the Buddha's power, the venerable Shariputra asked the noble and powerful Avalokiteshvara, the bodhisattva-mahasattva, "How should noble men and women, who wish to engage in the profound practice of transcendent wisdom, train?" Thus he spoke.

The noble and powerful Avalokiteshvara, the bodhisattva-mahasattva, answered the venerable Shariputra with these words: "Shariputra, noble men and women who wish to engage in the profound

45. The Transcendent Conqueror in the sutra itself refers to the Buddha Shakyamuni. The Lady Transcendent Conqueror of the sutra's title and opening homage refers to Prajñāpāramitā, Transcendent Wisdom, the dharmakaya that is the Great Mother of all realized beings.
46. A bhikshu is a fully ordained monk.

practice of transcendent wisdom should see this clearly: They should see clearly that the five aggregates are empty by nature.

"Form is empty, emptiness is form. Emptiness is not other than form; form is not other than emptiness. In the same way, feeling, discrimination, formation, and consciousness are empty.

"Thus, Shariputra, all phenomena are emptiness: They have no characteristics, no birth, no cessation, no stains, no freedom from stains, no decrease, and no increase.

"Thus, Shariputra, in emptiness there is no form, no feeling, no discrimination, no formation, no consciousness; no eye, no ear, no nose, no tongue, no body, no mind; no form, no sound, no smell, no taste, no tactile sensation, no phenomenon; no eye-faculty potential, no mental-faculty potential, no mental-consciousness potential, and nothing in between; no ignorance nor any ending of ignorance, no aging and death nor any ending of aging and death, and nothing in between.[47]

"In the same way there is no suffering, no origin of suffering, no cessation of suffering, no path, no wisdom, no attainment, and no nonattainment either. Thus, Shariputra, since for the bodhisattvas there is no attainment, they rely on and abide within transcendent wisdom, there are no obscurations in their minds, and they have no fear. They have gone far beyond error and have reached the ultimate transcendence of suffering. All the buddhas of the three times also rely on transcendent wisdom, and by doing so they fully and manifestly awaken into unsurpassable, complete, and perfect enlightenment.

"Thus, the mantra of transcendent wisdom, the mantra of great awareness, the unsurpassable mantra, the mantra of equality, the mantra that perfectly dissolves all suffering, should be known as true because it is not false. The mantra of transcendent wisdom is proclaimed:

47. "Nothing in between" refers to, with regard to the potentials, the fifteen potentials in between the eye faculty and the mental faculty; and with regard to the twelve links of dependent arising, the ten links in between ignorance and aging and death.

TE YA TA OM GA TE GA TE PA RA GA TE PA RA SAM GA TE BO DHI
SVA HA

"Shariputra, this is how bodhisattva-mahasattvas should train in profound transcendent wisdom."

Then the Transcendent Conqueror arose from that samadhi and praised the noble and powerful Avalokiteshvara, the bodhisattva-mahasattva, saying: "Excellent, excellent. Noble son, it is so. It is just so. Profound transcendent wisdom should be practiced just as you have taught. All the tathagatas rejoice."

When the Transcendent Conqueror said this, the venerable Shariputra, the noble and powerful Avalokiteshvara, the bodhisattva-mahasattva, the whole retinue, and the world with its gods, people, demigods, and gandharvas rejoiced and praised these words of the Transcendent Conqueror.

Thus ends the Mahayana Sutra called *Noble Lady, Transcendent Conqueror, Heart of Transcendent Wisdom*.

Appendix 3

THE TWENTY EMPTINESSES FROM CHANDRAKIRTI'S *ENTERING THE MIDDLE WAY*

INTRODUCTORY VERSES

Since selflessness is what liberates beings,
The Buddha taught two types: the selflessness of individuals and
  of phenomena.
Then, in order to better help those to be tamed,
The teacher taught further classifications. (179)[48]

In the extensive explanation of emptiness
There are sixteen classifications.
In the concise explanation the Buddha summarized these into
  four,
And these are explained to be the teachings of the Mahayana. (180)

1. Emptiness of the inner

Since it has no inherent nature,
The eye is empty of the eye.
Ear, nose, tongue, body, and mind
Are all described as being the same. (181)

They do not remain; they do not cease.
Therefore, the eye and the rest that are the six inner ones
Are things that have no inherent nature at all.
This is the "emptiness of the inner." (182)

---

48. Numbers in parentheses refer to the verse numbers from the sixth chapter of *Entering the Middle Way*.

2. Emptiness of the outer
Since their nature is emptiness
Forms are empty of forms.
Sounds, smells, tastes, tactile sensations,
And phenomena are exactly the same. (183)

Forms and so forth have no inherent nature:
This is the "emptiness of the outer." (184ab)

3. Emptiness of the outer and inner[49]
That both have no inherent nature
Is the "emptiness of the outer and inner." (184cd)

4. Emptiness of emptiness
Phenomena have no inherent nature—
The wise ones call this "emptiness."
It is asserted that this emptiness as well
Is empty of the essence of emptiness. (185)

The emptiness of what is called "emptiness"
Is the "emptiness of emptiness."
The Buddha taught it to counteract the clinging
Of the mind that thinks emptiness is a thing. (186)

5. Emptiness of the vast
Since they pervade everything without exception—
All sentient beings and the whole universe,
And since the immeasurables are an example of their infinitude,[50]
The directions are given the name "vast." (187)

---

49. "Outer and inner" refers to the meeting of the outer sources of consciousness (the subject of the second emptiness) with the inner sources of consciousness (the subject of the first emptiness) in moments of sense perception. The emptiness of this contact between outer and inner is the emptiness of the outer and inner.

50. The immeasurables are immeasurable love, compassion, joy, and equanimity for all sentient beings in the ten directions, which one cultivates as a part of Mahayana practice. The sentient beings in the ten directions are limitless in number, which is why these four contemplations are called immeasurable. That they are immeasurable for this reason is thus an example of the ten directions' infinite reach.

All these ten directions' emptiness
Is the "emptiness of the vast."
It was taught in order to reverse
Our clinging to the vast as being real. (188)

6. Emptiness of genuine reality

Nirvana is the supreme goal,
And therefore it is *genuine* reality.
Nirvana is empty of itself,
And this is the "emptiness of genuine reality." (189)

To counteract the mind's tendency to think that nirvana is a
   thing,
The Knower of Genuine Reality
Taught the "emptiness of genuine reality." (190)

7. Emptiness of the composite

Because they arise from conditions
The three realms are "composite," it is taught.
They are empty of themselves,
And this, the Buddha stated, is the "emptiness of the composite." (191)

8. Emptiness of the noncomposite

When arising, abiding, and cessation are not among its
   characteristics,
A phenomenon is "noncomposite."
These are empty of themselves,
And this is the "emptiness of the noncomposite." (192)

9. Emptiness of that which is beyond extremes[51]

That to which extremes do not apply
Is expressed as being "beyond extremes."

51. "That which is beyond extremes" refers equally to emptiness, dependent arising, and the Middle Way, because none of the extremes of permanence, extinction, realism, nihilism, existence, nonexistence, and so forth apply to or can describe their essential reality.

Its emptiness of its very self
Is explained to be the "emptiness of that which is beyond
    extremes." (193)

10. Emptiness of that which has neither beginning nor end
Since it has no point when it began
Nor time when it will end,
Samsara is called "that which has neither beginning nor end."
Since it is free from coming and going, it is like a dream. (194)

Samsaric existence is void of samsaric existence—
This is the "emptiness of that which has neither beginning nor
    end."
It was definitively taught in Nagarjuna's *Fundamental Wisdom of
    the Middle Way.* (195)

11. Emptiness of what should not be abandoned
To abandon something means
To throw it away or to get rid of it.
What should not be abandoned is
What one should never cast away from oneself—the Mahayana. (196)

What should not be abandoned
Is empty of its very self.
Since this emptiness is its nature,
It is called the "emptiness of what should not be abandoned." (197)

12. Emptiness of the true nature[52]
The very essence of the composite and everything else
Was not created by the students,[53] the solitary buddhas,
The bodhisattvas, or even the tathagatas. (198)

---

52. Emptiness is the subject of both the fourth and the twelfth emptinesses. The reason emptiness is described as being empty of its own essence twice is that we have two different ways of clinging to it. First, we cling to emptiness itself as being truly existent, and in order to reverse that, we are taught the emptiness of emptiness. Second, we hear the teachings that emptiness is the true nature of phenomena, and we then cling to this true nature as being truly existent. To reverse this type of clinging, we are taught the emptiness of the true nature.
53. "Students" refers to the shravakas.

Therefore, this essence of the composite and so forth
Is explained to be the true nature of phenomena.
It itself is empty of itself—
This is the "emptiness of the true nature." (199)

13. *Emptiness of all phenomena*[54]
The eighteen potentials, the six types of contact,
And from those six, the six types of feeling,[55]
All that has form and all that does not,
The composite and the noncomposite—these compose all
    phenomena. (200)

All of these phenomena are void of themselves.
This is the "emptiness of all phenomena." (201ab)

14. *Emptiness of defining characteristics*[56]
The nonexistence of entities such as "suitable to be form" and so
    forth
Is the emptiness of defining characteristics. (201cd)

All composite and noncomposite phenomena
Have their own individual defining characteristics.
These are all empty of themselves,
And this is the "emptiness of defining characteristics." (215)

15. *Emptiness of the imperceptible*
The present does not abide;
The past and the future do not exist.
Wherever you look, you do not see them,
So the three times are called "imperceptible." (216)

---

54. The emptiness of all phenomena is the emptiness of the names we give to things. For example, the name *fire* is empty of its own essence.
55. The six types of contact are the contact between the six inner sources of consciousness and their respective objects. The six types of feeling are the pleasant, unpleasant, or neutral sensations that arise as a result of the six types of contact.
56. The emptiness of defining characteristics is the emptiness of the bases to which we give names, for example, the emptiness of the actual thing that is hot and burning to which we give the name *fire*.

The imperceptible is empty of its own essence.
It does not remain, it does not cease,
And this is the "emptiness of the imperceptible." (217)

16. Emptiness of an essence in the nonexistence of things
Since things arise from causes and conditions,
They are mere collections that have no essence.
This nonexistence of collections is empty of itself,
And this is the "emptiness of an essence in the nonexistence of
   things." (218)

THE FOUR EMPTINESSES[57]

1. Emptiness of things
In short, "things" are
Everything included in the five aggregates.
These are empty of themselves,
And this is the "emptiness of things." (219)

2. Emptiness of the absences of things
In short, "absences of things" are
All noncomposite phenomena.
Absences of things are empty of themselves,
And this is the "emptiness of the absences of things." (220)

3. Emptiness of the true nature[58]
Phenomena's true nature itself has no essence—
This is the "emptiness of the true nature."
It is called "true nature"
Because no one created it. (221)

---

57. These four emptinesses are a summary of the first sixteen. The first two of the four
include all the phenomena in apparent reality and the latter two include everything in genuine reality.
58. This is the same as the twelfth emptiness above.

4. Emptiness of the other entity[59]

Whether or not buddhas appear in the world,
The natural emptiness of all entities
Is proclaimed to be
The "other entity." (222)

Other names for this are "genuine reality's ultimate limit" and
    "suchness"—
These are the "emptiness of the other entity."
These twenty emptinesses were taught extensively
In the *Sutras of Transcendent Wisdom.* (223)

---

59. Genuine reality is known as the "other entity" for three reasons: When compared with ordinary things it is supreme; it cannot be known by mundane consciousness but only by original wisdom; and in its nature it transcends everything in samsara.

Appendix 4

An Authentic Portrait of the Middle Way

From the standpoint of the truth that's genuine
There are no ghosts, there are not even buddhas,
No meditator and no meditated,
No paths and levels traveled and no signs,
And no fruition bodies and no wisdoms,
And therefore there is no nirvana there,
Just designations using names and statements.

All animate, inanimate—the three realms,
Unborn and nonexistent from the outset,
No base to rest on, do not coemerge,
There is no karmic act, no maturation,
So even the name "samsara" does not exist.

That's the way these are in the final picture,
But oh, if sentient beings did not exist,
What would the buddhas of three times all come from?
Since fruition with no cause—impossible!
So the standpoint of the truth that's superficial
Is samsara's wheel, nirvana past all grief.
It all exists, that is the Sage's teaching.

Then what exists appearing to be things,
And their nonexistence, reality that's empty,

Are essentially inseparable, one taste,
And therefore there is neither self-awareness
Nor awareness of what's other anywhere.

All of this a union vast and spacious,
And all those skilled in realizing this
Do not see consciousness, they see pure wisdom,
Do not see sentient beings, they see buddhas,
Don't see phenomena, they see their essence,
And out of this compassion just emerges
Retention, powers, fearlessness, and all
The qualities embodied by a buddha
Just come as if you had a wishing jewel—
This is what I, the yogi, have realized.

Glossary

ABHIDHARMA A set of the Buddha's teachings from the first turning of the wheel of Dharma in which he described the characteristics of, among other things, the sources of consciousness, aggregates, and dhatus. In these teachings, the Buddha did not explicitly refute the true existence of the phenomena that he described. He did explicitly refute their true existence, however, in the teachings of the second turning of the wheel.

AGGREGATES (*skandhas*, Skt.) The five groups of psychophysical phenomena—forms, feelings, discriminations, formations, and consciousnesses. Each individual sentient being is imputed to exist in dependence upon a unique collection of these skandhas. See Dependently arisen mere appearances.

ARHAT ("foe conqueror") A practitioner who has attained the fruition of either the Shravakayana or Pratyekabuddhayana by realizing the selflessness of the individual and thereby conquering the foe of the mental afflictions. By cultivating strong revulsion for and renunciation of samsara, and by perfecting their realization of the selflessness of the individual, the arhats completely free themselves from the mental afflictions and gain liberation from samsara. At a certain point, however, the buddhas wake them up from the peace of their meditative state, reveal to them that they have not yet attained the fruition of buddhahood itself, and exhort them to practice the Mahayana teachings for the benefit of all sentient beings. Doing so, they eventually attain the complete and perfect enlightenment of the buddhas.

BHAVAVIVEKA Indian master and author of a commentary on *The Fundamental Wisdom of the Middle Way* from the perspective of the Middle Way Autonomy school.

BHIKSHU A fully ordained monk.

BODHICHITTA "The mind turned toward supreme enlightenment." Bodhichitta has two aspects. The bodhichitta of apparent reality is the vow to lead all sentient beings to the state of the complete and perfect enlightenment of buddhahood. The bodhichitta of genuine reality is the true nature of reality itself, which, in the second of the three turnings of the wheel of Dharma, the Buddha explained to be emptiness beyond conceptual fabrication. In Mahayana Buddhist practice, one cultivates both types of bodhichitta.

BODHISATTVA "Courageous One of Enlightenment." A follower of the Mahayana path who cultivates the two types of bodhichitta. There are both ordinary bodhisattvas and noble bodhisattvas, the latter distinguished by their direct realization of the true nature of reality. Bodhisattvas are courageous because they take the vow to stay in samsara in order to benefit sentient beings, rather than seeking to escape from it.

BUDDHA The teacher; one who has attained complete and perfect enlightenment by perfecting the two qualities of the wisdom that realizes emptiness and compassion for all sentient beings.

BUDDHAPALITA Indian master and author of a commentary on *The Fundamental Wisdom of the Middle Way* from the perspective of the Middle Way Consequence school.

CHANDRAKIRTI Indian master and exponent of the Middle Way Consequence school, most famously in his commentary called *Entering the Middle Way*, which explains the meaning of *The Fundamental Wisdom of the Middle Way*.

COMPOSITE PHENOMENON Something that arises, abides, and ceases.

DEFINIENDUM That which is defined by a set of defining characteristics, for example, "fire."

DEFINING CHARACTERISTICS The set of characteristics that defines a particular definiendum, for example, "hot and burning."

DEPENDENTLY ARISEN MERE APPEARANCES The essential quality of all possible appearances there could be. Whatever it is, it can only arise in dependence upon its causes and conditions, and it is a mere appearance because it is empty of any inherent nature. The classic example is the moon that appears on the surface of a pool of water.

DHARMA The Buddha's teachings; the practice of these teachings.

DHATUS The Sanskrit term referring to two different groups of entities, translated as "elements" when referring to the six elements of earth, water, fire, wind, space, and consciousness; and as "potentials" when referring to a classification of eighteen phenomena. With regard to the elements, when the four great elements are mentioned, this refers to earth, water, fire, and wind; when the five elements are described, this refers to these four plus space; and when there are six elements, the last one is consciousness. With regard to the potentials, the eighteen are divided into three groups: the six outer potentials that are the objects of perception, namely, forms, sounds, smells, tastes, tactile sensations, and phenomena perceived by the mental consciousness; the six inner potentials that are the sense faculties that are the supports for perception, namely, the eye, ear, nose, tongue, body, and mind; and the six potentials that are the perceiving consciousnesses, namely, the eye, ear, nose, tongue, body, and mental consciousnesses. Mipham Rinpoche explains that what characterizes these eighteen is that each one possesses the ability or potency to perform its own specific function, hence the rendering into English as "potential."

DZOGCHEN "The Great Completion." A profound set of instructions that describes the true nature of reality and how to meditate upon it.

ELEMENTS See Dhatus.

EMPTINESS The true nature of phenomena, which is empty of the self of the individual sentient being, empty of true existence, and ultimately empty of any conceptual notion of what it might be, including the notion of emptiness itself.

FIVE POISONS See Mental afflictions.

FOUR NOBLE TRUTHS The main framework for the teachings given by the Buddha in his first turning of the wheel of Dharma, they present a basic outline of samsara and nirvana in terms of causes and results. The first, the truth of suffering, is the condition that pervades every aspect and every moment of existence in samsara. Second, the truth of the origin of suffering comprises the mental afflictions and karmic actions that are samsara's causes. Third, the truth of the cessation of suffering is nirvana, the state that is the transcendence of samsara's miseries. Fourth, the truth of the path comprises the teachings and practices that are the causes of attaining the truth of cessation and thereby gaining liberation from samsara.

GENDUN CHÖPEL One of the greatest scholars of modern times, he lived from 1902–1951.

GOTSANGPA An emanation of Milarepa and a great early master of the Drukpa Kagyu lineage, four generations removed from Lord Gampopa, Milarepa's most accomplished disciple.

JE TSONG-KHAPA (1357–1419) The founder of the Gelugpa lineage of Tibetan Buddhism.

JU MIPHAM RINPOCHE (1846–1912) A great master of the Nyingma lineage of Tibetan Buddhism and one of the leading figures in the Ri-me (nonsectarian) movement that began in Tibet in the middle of the nineteenth century.

KARMA/KARMIC ACTIONS *Karma* literally means "action," but it can also refer to the results of actions as well. The actions that ordinary sentient beings take with body, speech, and mind, motivated by one or more of the mental afflictions and which result in suffering, are known as karmic actions.

MACHIG LABDRÖN The greatest female practitioner in the history of Tibet, she gained her realization as a result of studying the sutras of the second turning of the wheel of Dharma.

MAHAMUDRA "Great Seal." A profound set of instructions that describe the true nature of reality and how to meditate upon it.

MAHAYANA The "Great Vehicle" of Buddhism, it is the path of the practice of the two types of bodhichitta, of wisdom and compassion together. Practitioners begin Mahayana practice by engendering the bodhichitta of apparent reality (see Bodhichitta), and then training in the six transcendent practices (*paramitas*): generosity, ethics, patience, diligence, concentration, and the wisdom that realizes emptiness, with the goal of attaining the enlightenment of the buddhas in order to lead all sentient beings to that same state.

MENTAL AFFLICTIONS (*kleshas*, Skt.) The disturbing states of mind that afflict ordinary sentient beings as a result of their not having realized the true nature of reality. The five main mental afflictions, also called the five poisons, are attachment or desire, aversion, stupidity, pride, and jealousy.

MIDDLE WAY The true nature of phenomena, lying in the middle between all possible extremes that can be conceived of by the intellect, including the extremes of existence and nonexistence, permanence and extinction, something and nothing, and even the notion of "middle."

MIDDLE WAY AUTONOMY SCHOOL (*Svatantrika Madhyamaka*) One of two branches of the Rang-tong Middle Way school. Its followers refute true existence and assert that emptiness is the true nature of reality.

MIDDLE WAY CONSEQUENCE SCHOOL (*Prasangika Madhyamaka*) One of two branches of the Rang-tong Middle Way school. Its followers refute true existence but do not assert that the true nature of reality is emptiness or anything else, because they realize that since genuine reality transcends all conceptual fabrications, to make an assertion about it would obscure the realization of its inconceivable essence.

MILAREPA The great yogi who was one of the founders of the Kagyü lineage of Tibetan Buddhism and who attained the state of buddhahood in a single lifetime.

NAGARJUNA Indian master, born four hundred years after the Buddha's passing, who authored commentaries on the Buddha's teachings in all three turnings of the wheel of Dharma.

NIRVANA "Transcendence of suffering," the liberation from samsara that is achieved, according to the Shravakayana and Pratyekabuddhayana, when one realizes the selflessness of the individual sentient being. According to the Mahayana, the only authentic nirvana is the state of buddhahood, which, due to the perfection of the wisdom that realizes the emptiness of all phenomena, does not fall into the extreme of samsaric existence and, due to the perfection of compassion, does not fall into the extreme of peace (as the nirvana achieved by the shravaka and pratyekabuddha arhats does).

NONAFFIRMING NEGATION A negation of existence that does not affirm the existence of anything in its place. For example, the statement "There is no spoon" merely negates the existence of a spoon without affirming the existence of anything else. This is opposed to an affirming negation, such as the statement "The lion is not dead." Negating death here implicitly affirms that the lion is alive.

NONCOMPOSITE PHENOMENON A phenomenon that does not arise, abide, or cease. There are three different noncomposite phenomena: space, the cessation that is the result of analysis, and the cessation that is not the result of analysis. The second refers to the absence of mental afflictions and suffering in the mindstream of an arhat who has realized the selflessness of the individual through analysis. The third refers to any cessation or absence of something that is not the result of the arhat's analysis; in other words, all the ordinary instances of the nonexistence or cessation of things that occur in the world on an everyday basis. For example, the nonexistence of elephants on the moon is an instance of this third type of noncomposite phenomena. All three of these share the common trait of being the absence of things that arise, abide, and cease. Noncomposite phenomena do not arise, abide, or cease because there is nothing there to arise, abide, or cease. They are the opposite of—the nonexistence of—things that do arise, abide, and cease.

POTENTIALS See Dhatus.

PRATYEKABUDDHAYANA "The vehicle of the solitary buddhas." One of two vehicles whose practices are based on the Buddha's teachings in the first turning of the wheel of Dharma. As a result of pride, followers of this path desire to attain realization by themselves, without a teacher or other students around. Thus, in their final lifetime as an ordinary sentient being, they are born in a place where the Buddhist teachings do not otherwise exist. Due to a certain set of circumstances, their past knowledge and habits awaken, and they are able to attain the state of arhat all by themselves, hence their name.

RANG-TONG SCHOOL The "empty of self" school, the branch of the Middle Way whose explanations are based on the Buddha's teachings from the second turning of the wheel of Dharma. It is composed of the Middle Way Autonomy and Middle Way Conseqence schools. Its name is derived from the explanation that phenomena are empty of their own essence—they are empty of whatever it is that they appear to be. For example, "The table is empty of the table" would be a statement this school would make, because when one subjects a table or any other phenomenon to logical analysis, the phenomenon cannot be found.

SAMSARA The cycle of existence in which sentient beings who do not realize the true nature of reality wander from one lifetime to the next, uninterruptedly experiencing suffering.

SANGHA In general, any community of Buddhist practitioners; in particular, the Sangha of realized noble arhats arcd bodhisattvas is the third of the three rare and supreme ones. This Sangha serves as one's guides and companions along the path of Dharma.

SHRAVAKAYANA "Vehicle of the Hearers." One of two vehicles whose practices are based on the Buddha's teachings in the first turning of the wheel of Dharma. Its name is derived from the quality of how intently its followers listen to the Buddha's teachings. The fruition of this vehicle is the attainment of the level of arhat.

SIDDHA "One who has gained accomplishment." A practitioner who has realized the true nature of reality.

SOURCES OF CONSCIOUSNESS (*ayatanas*, Skt.) There are six outer sources of consciousness: forms, sounds, smells, tastes, tactile sensations, and phenomena, which are the objects perceived by the six inner sources of consciousness: the eye, ear, nose, tongue, body, and mind.

THREE RARE AND SUPREME ONES The Buddha, Dharma, and Sangha, the three objects of refuge in the Buddhist tradition. One goes for refuge from the suffering of samsara to the Buddha, the teacher; the Dharma, the teachings to be put into practice; and the Sangha, the community of noble practitioners who have directly realized the true nature of reality and who serve as one's guides along the path. Also called the three precious jewels.

THREE REALMS The planes of existence inhabited by the sentient beings in samsara: the desire realm, the form realm, and the formless realm. The latter two are more subtle and are the exclusive domain of certain gods who have spent a long time cultivating specific meditative states of absorption. The desire realm is populated by all six classes of sentient beings: beings in the hell realms, hungry ghosts, animals, humans, and certain types of gods.

THREE STAGES OF THE BUDDHA'S TEACHINGS In the stage of no analysis, in order to guide his disciples to perform virtuous actions, avoid nonvirtuous ones, and give rise to the renunciation of samsara and longing for nirvana that would cause them to practice the Dharma, the Buddha described past and future lives, karmic cause and result, the suffering of samsara, and the liberation of nirvana as if they were all real, with no analysis of their true nature. In the stage of slight analysis, in order to help his disciples dispel their ignorance of genuine reality that caused them to believe in the true existence of appearances, the Buddha taught that all of the phenomena he described in the first stage do not truly exist and that emptiness of true existence is the true nature of reality. In the stage of thorough analysis, in order to help his disciples abandon their clinging to nonexistence, the Buddha taught that genuine reality transcends the conceptual fabrications of existence *and* nonexistence, appearance *and* emptiness, and any other notion of what it might be; it is beyond what the intellect can describe or conceive.

THREE TURNINGS OF THE WHEEL OF DHARMA The three sets of teachings that the Buddha gave. In the first turning, the Buddha taught that samsara is of the nature of suffering and that one can attain nirvana by practicing the Dharma. In the second turning, the Buddha taught that everything in samsara and nirvana is of the nature of emptiness. In the third turning, the Buddha taught about the buddha nature, the enlightened essence of luminous clarity that is the true nature of the mind of every sentient being.

VAJRAYANA "Adamantine vehicle." The set of Mahayana practices that is kept secret.

VINAYA The set of teachings the Buddha gave on the subject of prescribed and proscribed conduct for those who hold vows of the various *yanas* (vehicles) of Buddhism.

YOGI Literally, "one who arrives at naturalness." A practitioner who has directly realized the true nature of reality, to one degree or another. Thus, there are shravaka-yogis, pratyekabuddha-yogis, bodhisattva-yogis, and buddha-yogis, the last of these being the greatest yogis of all.

For more information about Khenpo Tsültrim Gyamtso's teachings, contact the Marpa Foundation at www.ktgrinpoche.org.